D1169496

Why Johnny
Can't Concentrate

Why Johnny Can't
Concentrate

Coping with Attention Deficit Problems

Robert A. Moss, M.D.

with Helen Huff Dunlap

B A N T A M   B O O K S

NEW YORK   TORONTO   LONDON   SYDNEY   AUCKLAND

WILLIAM WOODS UNIVERSITY

The information contained in this book is intended to complement, not substitute for, the advice of your own physician, with whom you should consult about your or your child's individual needs. You should always consult with your own, or your child's, physician before starting any medical treatment or medication. This is especially important if you or your child is already on any medication or under a physician's care.

Why Johnny Can't Concentrate
A Bantam Book / November 1990

All rights reserved.
Copyright © 1990 by Robert A. Moss, M.D. and Helen Huff Dunlap.
Cover design copyright © 1990 by One Plus One Studio.
Book design by Ann Gold.

No part of this book may be reproduced or transmitted
in any form or by any means, electronic or mechanical,
including photocopying, recording, or by any information
storage and retrieval system, without permission in writing from
the publisher.
For information address: Bantam Books.

Library of Congress Cataloging-in-Publication Data
Moss, Robert A., M.D.
   Why Johnny can't concentrate / Robert A. Moss with Helen Huff Dunlap.
      p.   cm.
   Includes bibliographical references (p. 203).
   ISBN 0-553-34968-6
   1. Attention.   2. Attention in children.   I. Dunlap, Helen.
   II. Title.
LB1065.M664   1990
153.1′523—dc20   90-404
                                                          CIP

Published simultaneously in the United States and Canada

Bantam Books are published by Bantam Books, a division
of Bantam Doubleday Dell Publishing Group, Inc. Its
trademark, consisting of the words "Bantam Books" and
the portrayal of a rooster, is Registered in U.S. Patent and
Trademark Office and in other countries. Marca Registrada.
Bantam Books, 666 Fifth Avenue, New York, New York 10103.

PRINTED IN THE UNITED STATES OF AMERICA

OPM   0 9 8 7 6 5

LB
1065
M664
1990

Contents

Acknowledgments

Our sincere thanks to:

Mead Johnson and Company for their grant;

Sydney Paver, Ph.D., of Austin Mental Health Associates,
who provided us with a great deal of advice and information for Chapter Eight;

Vicky Bijur, our agent, for believing in this book and helping in so many ways to make its publication possible;

Maria Mack and Michelle Rapkin, editors at Bantam
Books, who have given us valuable support and guidance;

Cynthia and Sara Moss, Bruce, Allison and Jeffrey Dunlap,
for their encouragement and patience throughout this project;

and all the parents and teachers who have been so concerned about this subject and so hungry for this information. This book is for you.

Foreword

Attention deficits are as puzzling and mysterious as they are potentially disabling to a developing child and his or her parents. Parents of children with attention deficits alternate between total exasperation over their child's carelessness and misguided actions to outright admiration for her or his incredible imagination and spirit. These children who so often grow up the hard way may ultimately perform and adjust far better as adults than they have as children. In the meantime, while watching and waiting for them to attain adulthood, we must strive to understand them, to avoid humiliating them, and to preserve and conserve their exciting strengths and affinities.

The traits associated with attention deficits are widely recognized. They include trouble concentrating, distractibility, difficulty getting satisfied, impulsivity, poor self-monitoring, and very confusing inconsistency. Although they share some traits in common, as a group children with attention deficits are extremely diverse. It is therefore inappropriate simply to lump them together and label them "ADD kids." Instead, we must acknowledge and celebrate their differences. We must try to observe, understand, and describe each child as an individual. At the same time, we must be careful not to dwell exclusively upon a child's deficiencies, especially since all children with attention deficits exhibit a multitude of remarkable strengths. Sometimes, in fact, the very same traits that cause them difficulty in childhood become transformed into assets later on in life. For example, a child who is highly distractible may become an incredibly creative adult, a person who notices things others would never notice, an individual who discerns relationships between things that would escape the notice of others. Similarly, a child who is extremely restless and insatiable throughout the school years may ultimately emerge as a highly ambitious adult, a person who keeps on wanting and who gets a large proportion of that which he or she wants!

Children with attention deficits also differ from each other with regard to those of their problems that seem to go along with their attention deficits. Most children who have attention deficits experience some form of learning difficulty during their school years. Their learning problems might include: deficiencies of memory, motor weaknesses, social skill deficits, language problems, and difficulties in specific subjects (such as mathematics or foreign language learning). Children with attention deficits are also likely to vary with regard to their emotional responses to the problem. Some show evidence of extreme anxiety or depression, while others display outstanding coping skills and are able to maintain a high level of self-esteem despite their attention difficulties.

The great diversity among children with attention deficits can lead to considerable confusion and professional disagreement. A child's patterns of behavior and learning may engender tremendous disagreement among clinicians, teachers, and parents. Because the problems of these children involve so many different areas of ability and behavior, it is often the case that a clinician can find what he was trained to find while evaluating a child with attention deficits! As a result, parents often have to contend with contradictory explanations offered by various teachers, school administrators, neighbors, relatives, and clinicians. The child too is likely to become exceedingly confused.

The only rational way to stem this tide of confusion is to have parents become much more sophisticated and educated in the subject of attention deficits. The present volume, written by a seasoned clinician, Dr. Robert Moss, will go far in meeting this objective. Based on his long experience in evaluating and treating children, Dr. Moss has been able to explain the various components of attentional dysfunction in such a way that parents can interpret what they see in their own children with much more clarity and sympathy. Dr. Moss realistically acknowledges the diversity of these children and the limitations of the labels (such as ADD and ADHD) that are used to categorize them. In addition, Dr. Moss offers some much needed suggestions regarding the everyday practical management of these needy youngsters. By reading this book, it is likely that parents will become much better consumers of services for their children with attention deficits. At the same time, they are likely to emerge as well-informed advocates whose love for their children is augmented by a firm commitment to preserve their strengths, to protect them from public humiliation, and to sustain their self-esteem by helping these children understand and appreciate themselves.

—DR. MEL LEVINE
CHAPEL HILL, N.C.

Why Johnny
Can't Concentrate

1.

An Introduction to Attention Deficit Disorder

Is your child easily distracted, disorganized, impulsive, and hard to satisfy? Is he or she temperamental, fidgety, or socially immature? Does your child remember countless trivial details but forget how to spell the words he spent two hours studying last night? Does the teacher say that your child can't sit still, has a short attention span, has trouble completing his assignments, or tends to daydream a lot? If a number of these characteristics rings a bell in your mind and seems to describe your son or daughter, then your child may have what is commonly referred to as attention deficit disorder.

Attention deficit disorder (ADD) is an inability to focus or concentrate. This attention impairment causes individuals to be easily distracted and poorly organized, and it often prevents them from achieving their full potential. These individuals may also exhibit any of the following: impulsivity, free flight of ideas, difficulty feeling satisfied, high activity level, social immaturity, mood swings, performance inconsistency, and memory dysfunction.

Children who have attention problems form a very diverse group—no two are alike. Some of these children have accompanying learning disabilities, some don't. Some have increased activity, while some even exhibit decreased or hypoactivity. Some have IQ's in the average range; others have intelligence that is well above or below average.

We encounter further diversity when we look at the causes of attention deficit. A small group of children with attention difficulties have a neurological disorder that may account for their poor concentration. Most attention deficit children, however, show no evidence of any central nervous system dysfunction. Many children with attention deficit have a family history of the problem, but others are the only members of their families to experience this difficulty. What all of these individuals do have in common is their inability to focus and concentrate, especially in a group setting.

Children with attention difficulties may have all kinds of trouble when they start school, because all stimuli carry equal weight with them—the teacher's voice, the dropped pencil, the closed book, the footsteps in the hall, and the noise from the playground. Individuals with attention deficit have trouble sorting out these stimuli and selecting which is the most important, making sustained attention next to impossible. For that reason, these individuals may experience failure both academically and socially. It is therefore essential that these children be spotted and helped as early as possible, before they begin to lose self-esteem and display behavioral difficulties.

A Common Problem

Attention deficit is a common problem. It has been estimated to comprise between 2.5 and 10 percent of the entire population (5 percent is the figure most frequently quoted). This means that there are approximately 15 million people who have attention deficit. In a typical classroom of twenty-five to thirty children, there is probably at least one student who has ADD, and, more often than not, that student is a male. A few years ago, we believed that the ratio of males with attention deficit to females with this problem was six or seven to one. Recent research has indicated that this figure was probably an exaggeration; more females have the problem than we once thought. In the past, females were less likely than males were to be diagnosed with attention deficit, because the females tended to be quieter, less active, and less disruptive in the classroom—today those stereotypical behavior patterns are changing. In addition, teachers, physicians, and parents are becoming better informed regarding attention deficit and more female students are being diagnosed with this problem.

Although knowledge of attention deficit is growing, there are still many misconceptions regarding this problem and its treatment. When we consider the tremendous number of people who have this difficulty, we can begin to see the need for all of us to have a greater understanding of this common and often undiagnosed problem.

A Look at Terminology

Throughout this book I will attempt to make some sense of the tremendous diversity found in individuals with attention deficit, without resorting to a lot of labels that have misleading connotations. Although I may occasionally use the term "attention deficit disorder" (ADD) in this book, I do not like the ring of the term "disorder," which seems to connote a more serious pathological problem. The term "disorder" implies that this is a disease with specifically defined characteristics that appear in every case. ADD does not have a list of distinct symptoms that will be present with each child. As we have seen, this condition encompasses a broad range of manifestations, and no two patients exhibit the same exact characteristics. For this reason, I will frequently refer to individuals who have ADD as having attention difficulties or attention deficit.

Looking at the history of this problem, we see terms such as "minimal brain damage" and "hyperactivity" misused to represent this large and varied group of individuals. The inaccuracies of these terms are readily apparent. We now know that, in the vast majority, there is no brain damage involved; except for the attention difficulty, most of these children's brains are just fine. The term "hyperactivity" is also misleading, because most children with attention deficit are not hyperactive.

Most recently, the *Diagnostic and Statistical Manual of Mental*

Disorders (third edition, revised) (DSM-III-R) has designated a new term, "attention deficit-hyperactivity disorder" (AD-HD). Unfortunately, in my opinion, this new terminology may add confusion, since most ADD children are not hyperactive.

With the increasing need for classifications of children's problems, both for the purposes of insurance and because of a need for a more systematic approach from health professionals, the terms "attention deficit disorder" (ADD) and "attention deficit disorder with hyperactivity" (ADDH) have been most frequently settled upon. Although recently changed, these are the terms that you will see most often in the literature you read.

How You Feel When Your Child Has Attention Deficit

Now that I have given you some basic information regarding attention deficit and the terminology that I will be using, I would like to address the issue of parenting a child with attention difficulties. If your child is having trouble in school, at home, with his peers, or in all of the above situations, you are probably extremely concerned. You may also feel frustrated because you don't know what to do to make things better.

Family members and friends offer all kinds of suggestions. Some of them might even blame you for your child's behavior. They say that you aren't "firm enough" and that you are spoiling your child. What they think the kid needs is a good spanking!

These people don't understand how difficult your child can be and how complicated it is to deal with him. They don't realize that physical punishment doesn't help; it just makes your child more aggressive.

It's hard not to listen to those close to you, and they have probably succeeded in making you feel guilty. You may blame yourself—at least partly—for your child's problems, and this feeling is normal. Even if others don't indicate that they blame you, it is perfectly natural for a parent to wonder if she or he is doing something wrong.

You also may feel some anger toward your child. You want her to respect and obey you. It's hard not to take some of her misbehavior personally. You can't help wondering why she is always testing you or embarrassing you, why she argues every time you tell her to do something, and why she is making your life so miserable.

Your anger may be so intense that at times it frightens you. You may worry that someday you will lose all patience and harm your child, either physically or emotionally—you may need to get some help soon to prevent that from happening.

On the other hand, it's possible that your situation is very different from the above scenario. Perhaps you don't have any major problems with your child at home—usually he's loving, cooperative, and obedient—it's just his schoolwork that worries you. You know your son is a very bright child, but his grades are not reflecting his intellectual capability. He rarely finishes an assignment, and the teacher says he's lazy.

However, you may be just as frustrated and upset as the parent whose child misbehaves at home. You desperately want your child to achieve in school, and you can't understand why he doesn't do better. You have offered all kinds of incentives for good work, but his grades haven't improved.

What Can You Do?

Whatever your child's problem may be, you can be assured that, by reading this book, you have taken the first step toward finding assistance. All kinds of help are available for children with attention problems, and this book will tell you how to find that help.

First of all, let me help you restore your faith in yourself and in your own ability to care for your child. If your child has attention deficit or a learning disability, it is not your fault. She is not a difficult child or a poor student because you have done something wrong, and you should not blame yourself for your child's problems. In fact, your love and support have probably prevented these difficulties from leading to something more serious.

Take heart, there is hope! Although there is no cure for attention deficit, there are many therapies that can help your child to improve behaviorally and academically. I can't promise you that everything will be perfect from now on, but I can tell you that things will get a lot better.

The initial step toward improving the quality of life around your house is for you to do everything within your power to determine the cause of your child's difficulties. I assume that you have some reason for believing that your child may have attention deficit, or you wouldn't be reading this book. Or, perhaps your child has already been diagnosed as having ADD, and you are avidly studying everything you can find concerning the problem. This book is for everyone who is interested in learning more about this complex condition that impairs concentration.

A Helpful Approach

In an attempt to enable readers to see some consistent patterns that may not have been apparent before, I have organized my discussion by age group. I want to point out from the beginning that, because this is such a diverse and interesting group of individuals, any classification pattern will have its drawbacks. I do believe, however, that this age-group approach provides the clearest method of describing the variety of children who display attention difficulties.

A recognition of the characteristics at different age levels can also go a long way toward eliminating much of the anxiety and guilt that physicians, teachers, and parents naturally feel when confronted with a problem that has been present for quite some time but was only clearly delineated at a particular age level. Perhaps the deficit was not noticed earlier because it impaired skills needed only at a certain period in the child's education.

Attention deficit problems surface at different stages of development with different children. The age at which a child begins to experience difficulties and display characteristic symptoms of ADD will depend on the severity of the attention deficit and the associated problems. Let me illustrate this point by giving you some sketches of children whose concentration problems have appeared at very different stages of development.

CHARLIE

At the age of four, Charlie has just been expelled from his second preschool. Teachers describe him as aggressive, temperamental, uncooperative, immature, and overactive. Charlie doesn't like to share or to wait for his turn to do anything. He takes what he wants, fighting for it if necessary. Charlie has violent temper outbursts that occasionally result in hitting, biting, or throwing things at other children or the teacher. He is extremely active, moving from one toy, game, or activity to the next. Charlie rarely sits still for stories or songs, and it is hard for him to complete a project.

Charlie has had problems at home, as well. He has never been an easy child. First, he was a colicky baby, a truly Terrible Two, and then a Threatening Three. He is now a Ferocious Four, and the forecast for age five doesn't look particularly promising.

Charlie has always been very stubborn and hard to satisfy. He screams or cries uncontrollably when he doesn't get what he wants, and a trip to the store with Charlie frequently turns into a nightmare.

Another difficulty is that Charlie can't deal with change. Even minor changes in his schedule or in his environment are enough to set him off. He hates almost anything that is new—babysitters, clothes, foods, furniture—because it is unfamiliar. He really prefers to wear the same clothes every day (even if they are filthy!), to sleep on the same sheets, and to eat the same foods. Despite his hyperactivity, Charlie sometimes gets locked into a particular project and may throw a fit when it is time for him to do something else. His parents don't know what to do with him. They argue a lot about discipline, and their marriage is beginning to suffer under the strain.

MICHELLE

Michelle is an intelligent second grader. She is a good reader with an impressive vocabulary, and her math skills are above average; yet, she is barely passing her school subjects.

Although she is a bright little girl, Michelle has a hard time retaining any new material presented in school. She struggles to get by academically and has a great deal of trouble with paper work. Michelle's handwriting is messy, her spelling poor, and it is hard for her to copy sentences from the chalkboard or a book. She often miscopies math problems, or she fails to pay attention to the symbol and uses the wrong procedure, adding instead of subtracting, for example. Michelle rarely finishes a written assignment, since she seems to do a lot of daydreaming and fidgeting. Although she doesn't get up from her desk very often and isn't disruptive, she just doesn't get much work done.

Because Michelle does occasionally succeed in completing an assignment, however, the teacher says that the child must be capable of doing better and has labeled her as either lazy or unmotivated.

Outside of school, things go much better for Michelle. She is a pleasant, cooperative child and has a happy home life. Socially, Michelle is rather immature, and she plays best with children who are younger than she is. She does have a few good friends who are her own age, though, and she seems to feel pretty good about herself.

JONATHAN

Jonathan is in the sixth grade, his first year of junior high school. He made good grades in elementary school without working very hard, but junior high is another story. The teachers require a lot of independent study. There are lengthy reading assignments, written and oral reports, and numerous projects. Jonathan can't seem to get all the work done, and, when he does finish assignments, he frequently misplaces them or forgets to turn them in. As a result, he is failing English, reading, and math, and everyone is getting on his case.

Jonathan had been given a placement test before school started. The examination had indicated that Jonathan was reading on a tenth-grade level, his math theory was on a seventh-grade level, his math computation skills were on an eighth-grade level, and his IQ was in the superior range. Yet he is failing sixth grade.

"Why aren't you doing better?" Jonathan's parents ask. "Why haven't you turned in your assignment?" his teachers ask. "We know you're capable of making better grades."

Jonathan is sick of all this. He is doing his best, but he can't keep up. He is mad at everyone for bugging him all the time, he's mad at himself for not being able to get his act together, and he's starting to think he's dumb.

Since he isn't passing anyway, Jonathan decides that he's wasting his time at school. He starts to skip classes and hang out at the apartments across the street from the school with some kids who seem to understand him.

Perhaps one of these children is the same age as your child and is experiencing some of the same problems. I hope that this recognition will mark the beginning of a new understanding of your child.

Looking at Children Who Have Attention Deficit by Age Groups

As I have said, all children with attention deficit are unique and begin to display their symptoms at different ages. A hyperactive child, a child with attention problems and accompanying learning disabilities, or a child with both attention deficit and a conduct disorder is likely to be diagnosed at an earlier age than a child who has simply a mild form of attention deficit. The following chart illustrates the approximate percentages of children with attention deficit who are diagnosed at different age levels:

18 months–5 years	5–11 years	11 years and older
20%	60%	20%

THE PRESCHOOLERS

In my experience in evaluating and treating hundreds of children with attention difficulties, I have found that the preschool group represents approximately twenty percent of the individuals assessed. It is interesting to note that most of the preschoolers I see with attention deficit are hyperactive. These hyperactive preschoolers are probably the easiest children with attention difficulties to diagnose because they have obvious symptoms. At the same time, they are the most difficult to treat. We must recognize, however, that the preschool child has tremendous variability in his developmental maturity. A four-year-old who may appear to be extremely hyperactive and headed for major behavioral and academic problems may seem much less problematic by the age of six.

Attention deficit with hyperactivity is generally the most severe form of attention deficit and thus can result in the greatest difficulty early on. For that reason, it is paramount to diagnose these children as soon as possible. These children can frustrate even the most supportive, caring family and need a lot of attention and guidance.

Approximately five percent of the children I diagnose display ADD symptoms at birth, if not before. These are the infants who kick in the womb and enter the world with bellowing that never seems to stop. Often, they are colicky and extremely difficult to console. These babies are rarely affectionate and are difficult to live with from Day One.

Another fifteen percent of the children diagnosed in my clinic have a fairly normal infancy, but once they enter the Terrible Twos, they never leave. These children are extremely active—always on the go and touching everything in sight. They end up in my office at age three or four because they are accidents looking for places to happen. They frequently get hurt, destroy things, act aggressively, and get thrown out of more than one preschool. They often have trouble winding down enough to go to sleep at night, and their tantrums and adventuresome antics can wreak havoc on a family.

EARLY ELEMENTARY SCHOOL CHILDREN

Over half of the children I evaluate and treat are in early elementary school. These individuals are usually not hyperactive, and they function adequately at home in a one-on-one situation. It is when they reach kindergarten and are required to pay attention in a classroom with twenty other children that they begin to suffer academically and/or socially due to their distractibility, impulsivity, and free flight of ideas. A child with a mild form of attention deficit may make it to first or second grade before experiencing difficulties.

LATE ELEMENTARY AND
JUNIOR HIGH SCHOOL CHILDREN

The final twenty percent of the children diagnosed with attention deficit are those who begin to have serious academic problems during late elementary school or in junior high school. Many of these students are very bright and have been able to get by in school by paying attention only twenty or thirty percent of the time. As their schoolwork becomes more advanced, requiring more independent study, these children lose the ability to compensate for their lack of concentration. Their grades may drop significantly, and teachers may refer them for counseling and testing.

HIGH SCHOOL STUDENTS AND ADULTS

Occasionally, high school students and adults are diagnosed with attention deficit. Most of those who are evaluated for attention deficit in high school or later have one of the three forms of ADD discussed above. For a variety of reasons, their attention deficit was not picked up until later in life. Perhaps these individuals had so much support from their families and teachers that they were able to make it through school without having any apparent concentration problems. Without this external organization, extra support, and remediation, these people probably would have displayed characteristic attention deficit symptoms at an earlier age.

An Overview of This Book

After giving you a general picture of the characteristics of attention deficit (Chapter Two) and the process of evaluation (Chapter Three), I will provide chapters that look at ADD in the three age groups outlined above: I will look at the preschoolers in Chapter Four, the early elementary school students in Chapter Five, and the late elementary and junior high youth in Chapter Six. I will examine the types of attention deficit in each age group and pinpoint specific characteristics that are common to children whose attention problems become apparent at a certain age. Later in the book, in Chapter Eleven, I will talk about attention problems in adults, because it is likely that some of the adults who read this book will have attention deficit themselves.

The remainder of the book will be devoted to providing you with specific information that will equip you to do everything you can to help your child and to find qualified professionals who will be able to give additional support if needed. In Chapter Seven, I will discuss medical treatment for attention deficit, looking carefully at the various medications that are appropriate for treating children of different ages and with varying attention difficulties. I will also talk about some inappropriate fad therapies which can be a waste of your time, money, and hopes. Chapter Eight will focus on the parent's role in treating attention deficit with behavior modification techniques. Chapters Nine and Ten will discuss educational therapy for children with attention difficulties, looking at the roles of both the parent and teacher in the child's learning. Finally, in Chapter Twelve, you will find some recommendations regarding how to find the best assistance for your child and for yourself. I will talk about medical professionals, counseling, parent support groups, national associations, and publications.

Your child and his or her attention difficulties present a unique challenge and this is the book that will help you to meet that challenge head-on. It will guide you to a better understanding of your child's personality and behavior, and it will get you started on a program that will help you feel more positive in your dealings with your child.

2.

Characteristics of Attention Deficit

Whether or not your child has been diagnosed with ADD, you are probably interested in learning more about the characteristics or symptoms of attention deficit. When you realize that some of his or her behavior is due to attention problems and is not intentional, it will change the way you feel about and deal with your child's actions.

I would encourage you to look carefully at the following information and apply it to your child, but I would strongly discourage you from attempting to make any diagnosis yourself. Attention problems are extremely complex and need to be evaluated by a team of professionals, which we will discuss in greater detail in later chapters.

The characteristics of children with attention deficit include a very broad range of behaviors, depending on both the child's age and the severity of the attention problem. A child with attention deficit will display some of the characteristics that I discuss, but not all of them. Each child who has an attention deficit problem is unique; his symptoms are influenced by his personality and environment.

Interestingly enough, those characteristics that are usually present may not be exhibited every day. A child who is frequently inattentive may occasionally concentrate beautifully. Even a child with a severe form of attention deficit will have a good day at school every now and then—one of the most consistent things about these children is their inconsistency.

I must also point out that, on any given day, one or more of the attention deficit characteristics may be present in any child—or in any adult, for that matter. Each trait should therefore be viewed as a symptom that may or may not have relevance, depending on the age of the child, time of onset, and associated problems. In diagnosing an attention deficit, I find the patterns and the presentation of characteristics in each individual child to be more significant than the presence or lack of certain behaviors. The following are the six most common symptoms of attention deficit disorder:

Primary Characteristics

1. *Short attention span and distractibility.* The two main ingredients of attention deficit are a short attention span and distractibility which are very closely related. A child with a short attention span is going to be easily distracted, but this child can have a short attention span even when there is no external factor to distract him. He may just fail to concentrate on one activity because he is *choosing* to do, or to think about, something else.

When a stimulus is presented to the brain, one can choose to ignore or to respond to that stimulus. Recognition of how much of this ability is in our conscious control and how much is subconscious is at the heart of understanding many of the characteristics of attention deficit.

We have made great strides toward understanding what is actually going on inside the brains of children with attention deficit. Since individuals recovering from head injury or infectious illness display impulsivity and hyperactivity, it was once thought that hyperactive children must have some form of minor brain injury. This led to the first medical term for attention deficit, "minimal brain damage," which was used in the 1950s and 1960s.

Fortunately, as our knowledge has increased, it has become readily apparent that the vast majority of individuals with attention deficits have perfectly normal brains, and, indeed, most are not even hyperactive. So why is there a similarity to the restless, impulsive, distractible behaviors that we see in people with brain damage? The answers are slowly becoming evident.

In the past ten years, there has been a great deal of research both in Danish medical literature as well as from the National Institute of Mental Health in Bethesda, Maryland. Many of these studies have used a new type of brain scanner called the positron emission tomography (PET) scan, which provides us with sophisticated information about the various parts of the brain and their functions. From these studies we have learned that a certain part of the brain, the frontal lobe, is directly involved in controlling attention, activity, and the ability to plan ahead. It is not responsible for intelligence, however, which is compatible with our knowledge that the vast majority of children with attention deficits have normal intelligence.

We are just beginning to understand how all this fits together. It certainly makes sense that individuals who have had major brain injuries or infections that have affected their frontal lobes experience impulsive, inattentive behaviors. We also know that more than ninety-five percent of the individuals with attention deficits have not had any brain damage.

Although there are still many theories as to the cause of attention problems, there has recently been much scientific support for a neurophysiological explanation. When a brain cell is stimulated, it releases a neurotransmitter that carries the message to the next cell. The neurotransmitter attaches itself to the cell, causing that cell to be stimulated. Then another messenger is released. All of this happens in a split second, which allows the message to travel quickly from one cell to the next along what we call neuropathways. There are thousands of these pathways that carry messages to specialized areas of the brain.

Several stimuli may be competing for our attention at once, since we see, hear, and feel all at the same time. Therefore we sometimes have to make a concerted effort to concentrate. Right now, you are reading these words and thinking about what all this means. You may be aware of the sound of a lawn mower outside or voices from another room, and you may even have a slight headache, but you are still able to focus on your reading. It seems that, when we have to work to concentrate, our brain releases extra neurotransmitters. These additional messengers cause the messages to travel a little more quickly and enable us to focus, concentrating on one area and blocking out other stimuli. In this way, neurotransmitters have a responsibility for behavior and learning, and a deficiency can have profound effects on an individual's ability to function normally. People who have attention deficit do not seem to manufacture extra neurotransmitters. All messages come in at once with equal velocity. The brain becomes like the telephone system on Mother's Day when wires get overloaded and messages cannot reach their destinations.

Most individuals with attention deficit are born with this shortage of neurotransmitters, which tends to run in families, primarily on the male side. A small percentage of attention deficit cases are caused by severe damage to the brain. This damage could result from serious birth trauma, severe head injury, or meningitis in childhood. These cases, however, are a small minority of the attention deficits; most people with ADD have normal brains and average intelligence.

Why this shortage affects only the frontal lobe is an unanswered question. Again, some recent research has indicated that other areas of the brain may also be involved. One of these is the reticular activating system, which is found in the brain stem; this area is also influenced by neurotransmitters.

The neurophysiological explanation of attention deficit has been directly related to the theory behind stimulant medication to treat this problem. This was once referred to as a "paradoxical effect," since people wondered how a stimulant could "slow down" a child who was physically or mentally hyperactive. We now think that the stimulant medication increases the production or release of neurotransmitters, allowing the child to focus on the most important message being sent.

An understanding of the basic physiology involved is critical if we are to truly understand this phenomenon of attention deficit and attempt to assess children with learning difficulties. It is also essential to note, as I emphasized in my introduction and will continue to stress throughout this book, that children with attention difficulties are a widely diverse group. They are likely to differ from each other in symptoms, intelligence, and styles of learning. They may also vary in the sources of their problems, their responses to different forms of therapy, and the degree of support they receive from their families. Attention deficit will have a different effect upon each individual's choice of career, spouse, and social interaction.

In addition to the physiological aspects of attention deficit, there are other properties that must be taken into consideration. We must look at the fundamental properties of the stimulus—the place, the color, the size, the shape, etc. We must also consider the emotion linked to the stimulus, other patterns associated to the stimulus, and, probably most importantly for school-age children, any competing stimuli. The ability to separate all these out and focus on the most important stimulus coming in at any one time is the key.

Certain stimuli will take precedence. A loud firecracker or a sudden bolt of lightning will get everyone's attention. Pain, whether physical or emotional, will also compete strongly for attention. We all experience difficulties with concentration at various times and for various reasons. The individual with attention deficit has a more chronic concentration problem. He may be too active either physically or mentally to settle down sufficiently for the completion of a task.

Children with attention deficit will inevitably experience some degree of difficulty in school due to their poor concentration. They will have trouble listening to lengthy instructions or lectures, and they will often be unable to concentrate on reading or written assignments long enough to complete a task. As I mentioned earlier, their short attention span is frequently, but not always, due to distractibility. Sometimes, even when there is nothing to distract a child, she just can't concentrate.

Children who have attention difficulties do tend to display a tremendous level of distractibility. This particular characteristic is related to the inability to effectively modulate the variety of stimulation that is entering the brain at any one time. We have a specialized area of the brain that accepts only visually presented material. Entering the brain at the same time could be auditory material going to another specialized area, as well as sensory phenomena entering a third section of the brain.

With an inability to regulate these various stimuli, it becomes almost impossible for children with attention deficit to focus consistently on the most important stimuli, which, in the classroom, generally come from the teacher. These children may be listening very intently one minute, when suddenly they notice a friend out on the playground. They become distracted and begin to stare intently out of the window, forgetting entirely what the instructor is discussing. Often the focus of attention may be totally irrelevant, such as a crack in the wall, the noise of a clock moving, the air-conditioner, etc.

Distractibility frequently becomes a more serious problem during the late elementary and junior high school years, when there is less repetition in the classroom, and a greater amount of independent work is required. Individuals with attention deficit have made the analogy of it being like trying to watch television with four channels on the screen at the same time. It would be next to impossible to make any sense out of a bombardment of stimuli, and this may be exactly what children with attention difficulties face on a daily basis in a classroom setting.

2. *Impulsivity*. Equally important as distractibility, is impulsivity. In the most elementary terms, impulsivity is simply acting before thinking. Individuals with attention deficit, due to their concentration problems, simply do not take the time to contemplate the consequences of many of their actions.

For young children, impulsivity may result in a series of injuries. These kids often leap before they look—literally as well as figuratively. A young child with attention problems may jump from a roof just because it looks like fun. He may also experience frequent altercations with friends because of his impulsive words and actions.

The effect of impulsivity is most significant socially. Children with attention deficit generally fail to inhibit inappropriate actions, often being totally unaware of the social consequences of these actions. With this inability to successfully predict the outcomes of their actions, children who have attention deficit often create repeated behavioral offenses both in and out of the classroom. They tend to want to be in charge of all social interactions, and they may annoy others by their attempt to dominate. These children seek to take charge, because this dominance allows them to move quickly from one interaction to another so they don't become bored.

In the classroom, these children may stand out because of their impulsive behavior. They may constantly interrupt the teacher, jumping up to answer a question before it is even asked. They are likely to work impulsively on paper, jotting down answers without thinking problems through and without taking the time to read questions thoroughly. In addition, students with attention deficit may aggravate others because of their aggressiveness.

The socialization problem may increase in adolescence, when these individuals often want to test speed in cars, highs from alcohol and drugs, and sex without planning or protection. Male teens with attention deficit may be more likely to get girls pregnant than their counterparts who have no attention problems. Females with attention deficit may be more likely to become pregnant than their friends. Much of this is due to impulsivity: young people with attention difficulties rarely stop to consider the consequences of their actions. This, of course, may carry over into adulthood.

It is interesting that, one-to-one, you can often reason with children who have attention deficit and help them to logically predict the consequences of their actions. However, in a group this ability seems to be overwhelmed, and they resume acting first and thinking later. Delayed gratification is a foreign concept to these impulsive children; they don't consider future rewards or punishments when they get ready to act.

3. *Free flight of ideas.* This characteristic of attention deficit is related to distractibility. When a child has attention deficit, things

are continually popping into her mind and she has a hard time sorting out what is important and what's not. Distractibility can lead to persistent daydreaming, where one word or idea will result in a complete train of thought that is totally irrelevant to what is going on at the particular time. A child who has attention deficit may be listening to the teacher and hear the word "Colorado." This may bring to mind last winter's ski trip and what her uncle taught her on the slopes. The child may then start thinking about her uncle's new home in California. Five minutes after the mention of Colorado, the teacher may ask that child a question, and the child will have no idea what the teacher is talking about or what has been said for the past five minutes.

Due to distractibility and free flight of ideas, the child with attention deficit often seems to be in another world, and it is important for parents and educators to understand that this is no one's fault. The child does not choose to tune anyone out—this has little to do with the quality of instruction or even the child's interest in what is being said. The focus of attention changes so rapidly and ideas come so fast that the child often finds it impossible to concentrate, despite her good intentions. Even when the child who has attention deficit is not physically hyperactive, she may indeed be mentally hyperactive.

With this free flight of ideas and impulsivity, the child who has attention difficulties often tends to take over a conversation, interrupting frequently and calling out in large group discussions. She may be afraid that she will lose an idea if she doesn't voice it immediately. There is also the possibility that this individual, in an attempt to focus on one thought, may forget everything else, including classroom rules or social etiquette. She frequently annoys others by unintentionally saying things that are unkind. Sometimes, she is thinking faster than she can talk, and the words don't come out quite right. She may not even be aware that she's offended someone or broken a rule.

This child may also make comments that seem totally unrelated to the subject at hand. Because of her "hyperactive" thought process and free flight of ideas, she has arrived at a thought that seems perfectly logical to her, and, if pressed, she could probably explain how she got there.

Such a child can be very frustrating to deal with, but we must remember that this is characteristic of attention deficit and is not something that the young child can control. This free flight of ideas, as we have seen, can seriously hinder a child's concentration on a task and can get her into all kinds of trouble. In Chapters Eight and Ten, I will offer some suggestions that may help adults in getting and keeping the attention of the child who has trouble concentrating.

4. *Poor organizational skills.* The next important characteristic we see in looking at children with attention difficulties seems to be poor organizational skills. Because of their inability to focus on any one activity long enough, these children have an extremely difficult time coordinating all the tasks in a particular activity. Children with attention deficit invariably have messy school desks with materials in every corner, making it most difficult for them to find anything they need. (This, incidentally, often carries over to their rooms at home, where toys, books, and clothes may cover the floor, and one enters at one's own risk!)

Children who have attention deficit have been known to struggle to complete an assignment, and then after a lot of hard work and effort, lose it before it ever gets to the teacher's desk. The idea of writing down a homework assignment, taking the right book home, completing the assignment, taking it to school the next day, and then turning it in, is incomprehensible to them. I have had dozens of parents tell me that they attempt to control every step of that process, from seeing that the child gets the work home and completes it, to putting the work in the notebook, only to have the child leave the notebook in a locker the next morning and not turn the assignment in to the appropriate class that day.

Because of the increased need for organizational skills as school becomes more complex, we find that organization becomes extremely important for junior high school students. When children start changing classrooms for different subjects, they become responsible for their study materials. They must move their school supplies from one class to another. Keeping track of all their books, folders, papers, pencils, and pens—as well as the gym clothes, jacket, lunch bag, and musical instrument—can be a monumental task for preteens with attention deficit.

In addition to organizing their belongings, these students are required to organize their thoughts to a much greater degree than in elementary school. They begin to write more outlines, essays, and reports, and they are called upon more frequently to make speeches. Students who have attention deficit may experience difficulty with such assignments; in fact, poor organization may be the primary symptom in the junior high age group.

This organizational difficulty seems to be pervasive, carrying on into adulthood. An individual with attention difficulties must often set up a system that imposes some external controls to assist in the organization process. Appointment calendars, check-off lists for chores and errands, and written goals are helpful for many people, and are essential for disorganized adults who have attention deficit. Naturally, adults have more cognitive skills than young teenagers do, and it's this cognitive sophistication that enables adults with attention deficit who have been supported throughout their elementary and secondary school years to use whatever strategies they need to organize their lives.

5. *Insatiability.* Another characteristic that we often find in children with attention problems is insatiability. This characteristic is often seen in younger children, and it sometimes, but not always, becomes less significant as they mature. Insatiability is an unquenchable desire. The insatiable child will crave something to the exclusion of anything else in the world at that particular moment. Unfortunately, this intense desire is rarely satisfied for long. Even when these children manage to get what they want, they may not be content. A short time later they may want something else with equal intensity, and usually these children are chronically dissatisfied no matter what is done for them.

An insatiable child with attention deficit may throw a screaming fit in a grocery store because he is hungry. After his mother gives him the granola bar she has placed in her purse for that purpose, he may eat it and then have a raging tantrum over a toy he can't live without. Since children who have attention deficit are often egocentric and characteristically restless, insatiability can frequently lead to significant mood fluctuations as well. Insatiability is not as common as the characteristics referred to previously, but it can be quite overwhelming when present.

6. *Hyperactivity.* The sixth characteristic associated with these children is particularly interesting, since it was previously considered the hallmark of a child with attention deficit. This characteristic, hyperactivity, is nothing more than the inability of the central nervous system to effectively modulate motor activity. A significant fact about hyperactivity is that it really affects less than thirty percent of the individuals with attention deficit. That is an extremely interesting point, since for many years the entire attention deficit syndrome was referred to as hyperactivity.

Hyperactivity can range anywhere from some minor fidgetiness, when a child is under stress in a group or a class, to overt hyperkinesis, when the child is in perpetual motion from getting out of bed in the morning to going to sleep at night. Even in sleep, hyperactive children are often restless, and their sleep cycles tend to be very short.

The unfortunate thing about this hyperactivity is that it is rarely focused. A hyperactive child tends to move from one item to the next with very little purpose extended to any of this activity. Usually the activity level rises with increased stimulation in the surrounding environment. A simple activity, such as a trip to the grocery store, can be truly an adventure with a hyperactive child. A trip to a busy shopping mall, with a child running in three directions at once and touching everything in sight, can be total chaos for all concerned.

Hyperactive children often start out extremely demanding, with very poorly developed sleep patterns even as infants. Mothers of these children frequently relate that the children never learned to walk; they simply started to run and indeed never stopped. Everything in the house that was not nailed down was turned over or taken apart at some point. Hyperactive children are in perpetual motion and rarely, if ever, rest, which can be trying to even the most patient parents.

Interestingly enough, as noted earlier, most children with attention deficit do not have this characteristic, and those who do seem to "grow out of it." This is not true with most of the other characteristics of attention deficit that we have discussed. Those characteristics are usually much more pervasive and can often persist into adulthood. However, hyperactivity and insatiability do seem to moderate a great deal as a child enters adolescence.

Secondary Characteristics

The characteristics outlined above are probably the most important aspects of attention deficit, but there are a number of secondary characteristics that may be prevalent in certain individuals. How these exactly fit into the overall scheme of attention deficit will be better defined when we discuss the different characteristics of individuals with attention deficit at different ages.

1. *Social immaturity.* Many children with attention deficit problems are socially immature. Much of their social immaturity is directly related to earlier characteristics. Because they are so distractible, they often have a difficult time picking up on social cues and thus fail to learn many of the social nuances essential in early elementary school for peer acceptance. Accompanying this are their impulsivity and insatiability, which often come across as strange and unacceptable behaviors to their peers and can be very frustrating for both the parents and the child. The sense of social isolation often makes these children try harder, which only serves to perpetuate the problem. Children with attention difficulties appear to be continually testing their peers, their teachers, and their parents.

2. *Performance inconsistency.* The next characteristic we occasionally find in children with attention difficulties is performance

inconsistency. Many of these children can vary tremendously from day to day in their level of activity or ability to concentrate to the point that everybody is ready to blame their behavior on anything, from what they ate for breakfast to the cola that they consumed last Tuesday. In a vast majority of cases, such things as diet have little or nothing to do with this inconsistency.

One day a child with attention deficit can finish all the assignments and remember which book to bring home; then for the next two weeks she may not get any of this straight. She may be extremely motivated one day and make an A on every assignment. Then, for the next three days, she won't receive a grade above a C. I am not exactly sure why this tremendous inconsistency occurs, but it does, and I see it in many children with attention deficit.

Inconsistency is frustrating to all, especially to the child, and unfortunately leads to the child's hearing over and over again, "I know she can do it, since I've seen her do it in the past. She must not be trying." Or, a child may hear, "She obviously has the ability to get her work done. She only lacks motivation." The problem breeds frustration and anxiety for the child, as well as for the parents and instructors.

3. *Inflexibility.* Some of these children with attention deficit may be extremely inflexible and have a difficult time tolerating change. With a compelling need to stick to daily routines and patterns, these children may react to alterations with tantrums and other immature behavior. They may have severe separation problems in the early years and throw fits when left at preschool or with a babysitter. Even slight changes in daily routines, such as a trip to the doctor, may lead to violent tantrums that may take an hour or more to settle down. This can even occur when a child has had warning of a trip or appointment.

Minor changes in room furnishings may be particularly upsetting for some children with ADD. Many children who have attention difficulties are likely to be unhappy with new furniture or appliances; they are much more comfortable if things remain the way they are. Even a preteen with attention deficit may resist the replacement of her childhood bedspread, saying that it is "special" to her. Don't be surprised if your child is not enthusiastic about selling her old toys, clothes, and furniture at a garage sale.

This leads to the subject of moving. A move is never easy with children, and the experience can be particularly difficult for children with attention deficit. They may desperately miss their old home—old bedroom, living room, kitchen, and back yard. They may also cry over missed friends for months. Their inflexibility makes the transition to a new home and community quite an emotional one, but parents can be assured that the tears will dry. Eventually, these children become as firmly attached to their new setting as they were to the old.

4. *Mood swings.* The emotional state of a child with attention difficulties may be marked by inconsistency. Some of these children may display tremendous mood swings from heights of hilarity to depths of despair, laughing hysterically one minute and crying inconsolably the next. Due to their frequent frustration and poor self-esteem, they may also experience periods of depression. Children whose attention problems remain undiagnosed and untreated may come to perceive themselves as "bad" or "dumb" and may misbehave in order to get attention. They may also be quick-tempered and prone to explosive outbursts of anger or physical aggression.

These children may be very difficult to work with or live with, and they need a great deal of love, understanding, and positive reinforcement. It is important for parents to remember that children with ADD frequently act the way they do because of their attention problem: their misbehavior isn't always their fault. They usually don't plan to hit or bite their friends, and in most cases they don't plot against parents or siblings. They do what they feel like doing at a given moment without considering the repercussions. Adults can help these children by providing calm, firm, consistent discipline when necessary, and by rewarding them when they do manage to exhibit self-control.

5. *Poor short-term memory*. Many children with attention problems have selective memory dysfunction, which, again, is frustrating for the adults dealing with these children. Individuals with attention deficits often fill up their minds with insignificant details. A child who has attention deficit may be able to describe every detail about the dress and hat that Aunt Clara wore to a wedding two summers ago but won't be able to remember the sum of two plus two. For example, a seven-year-old patient of mine recently saw my newly grown mustache and remembered that I had worn a mustache three years earlier. The child's mother was astounded at this recall, since he can't remember how to spell a word with more than three letters.

This short-term memory dysfunction, along with tremendous distractibility, makes it very difficult for children with attention deficit to follow more than one direction at a time. Telling them to complete two or three tasks at once is often an exercise in futility, leading to inevitable distraction. For example, a child who is told to go to her room, put on her socks and shoes, and find her library book may find one sock and then be distracted when she sees her favorite doll, forgetting all about the other tasks.

The memory problem becomes even more frustrating and pervasive as these children enter junior high and high school, where the demands for memory become much more stringent. Spelling and vocabulary lists become much more difficult, and the drilling of words is greatly reduced. Students are expected to recall numerous facts in all subjects, and much of this memorization is likely to be extremely troublesome for the student with attention deficit.

Other Characteristics

There are many other characteristics that are seen in certain children with attention difficulties. Some of these students experience fine motor (small muscle) and writing problems, while others have trouble with gross motor (large muscle) coordination. Some have poor sleep-wake cycles, where they are constantly fatigued—they yawn, but don't really want to go to sleep.

Many have domineering social behavior and a compelling need to be the center of attention and in control of the activity at all times.

Knowing how this wide variety of characteristics blends in is essential in understanding this process. Many of these characteristics are very common in children at certain ages but manifest themselves in different ways as the children mature. Looking at these traits and checking them off in one's mind ("Yes, my child has this," and "No, my child does not have that") is an important first step, but further steps must be taken.

It is necessary to have each child evaluated and to see how his or her overall presentation is related to the inability to modulate and focus attention. After obtaining a neurophysiological assessment, accompanied by the complete evaluation of both the educational and psychological functioning of a child, you will have a much clearer understanding as to whether your child's particular symptoms are consistent with attention deficit disorder.

Once you have more information regarding your child's problem, a curtain will be lifted and a whole new world of support will be open to you. There is a host of professionals who are capable of helping you and your child, and there are many parents who have had experiences like yours and will be there for you every step of the way. Life will not always be a rose garden, but you'll have a lot of help pulling the weeds!

3.

Diagnosing
Attention Deficit

I know that your child's problems have been very frustrating. You love your child and want him or her to succeed in school and have friends. You wish for a happy home life. Things will improve: you are on your way toward helping your child and reducing the tension in your household.

First of all, you need to know for certain what is causing your child's academic, psychological, or behavioral problems. If, after reading the first two chapters of this book, you think that your child may have attention deficit, you need to have your child fully evaluated. ADD, as I have said before, is an extremely complex problem. The diagnosis must be made by professionals.

A Threefold Approach

Unfortunately, there is no single, simple test that can be used to diagnose attention deficit. No blood test or brain scan or checking off of characteristics on a behavioral form can prove that a child has ADD. Diagnosis can be made only after thorough educational, psychological, and medical testing. I strongly recommend all three types of evaluation. Because of the diversity of the characteristics found in children with attention deficit, and because there are other problems that mimic this disorder, I believe that the educational, psychological, and medical aspects of this problem must all be examined. You will find groups that look at only one aspect of attention deficit and offer a strictly medical, psychological, or educational approach to diagnosing and treating the problem. Personally, I find these limited programs to be only minimally effective.

As a result, my learning evaluation center chooses to use the following team approach for a more comprehensive evaluation:

EDUCATIONAL ASSESSMENT
The first member of the team is an educational therapist who needs to do a thorough assessment of the child's IQ, or intellectual potential, as well as his or her achievement level in comparison with peers. If a large discrepancy between these two, or between a child's IQ and achievement in actual academic grades· is found, we must look for the source of this discrepancy.

Most children with attention deficit display IQ scores that are somewhat deflated due to their difficulty concentrating. This results in a decrease in factual attainment as well as an inability to focus on areas of the test itself when sustained attention is required. However, despite this underestimate of IQ, these children often show a discrepancy between intellectual ability and achievement in school, since school achievement is even more adversely affected.

It also may be helpful to look at the profile of the Wechsler (the most common IQ test) in an effort to spot profiles that point to attention difficulties, as well as special weaknesses that may suggest a particular form of learning disability. Certain subtests of the Wechsler require more sustained attention than others, and children with attention deficit tend to display lower scores in these areas; your educational therapist can help you with this.

We can thus see that, although this educational information is not diagnostic in itself, it does provide an important piece of the puzzle in looking at these children.

PSYCHOLOGICAL ASSESSMENT
The second essential member of the team is a clinical psychologist or social worker one can consult if necessary to adequately

assess both the child and the family from a behavioral perspective. Many children with attention deficit can experience some secondary behavioral and emotional problems. The severity of these problems will depend on how long the child has dealt with his or her frustration and academic difficulty. Much of this also appears to be related to the degree of that particular child's attention problem and how significantly it has interrupted the child's normal peer relationships. Since attention deficit has a potential for taking its toll on a child's self-esteem, a psychological evaluation is often crucial.

Attention deficit can also raise havoc in a family. A child who is having trouble in school, and is also making disproportionate demands on your family is hard to care for. Parents often feel guilty and angry, and spouses may have serious disagreements regarding the handling of the child.

It should also be noted that, if we are truly dealing with an attention deficit, there is usually a history of this in other family members. If ADD was not discovered and adequately treated in his or her youth, an adult may display counterparts to the characteristics seen in children with attention deficit problems, adding to the instability of the family system.

Family problems compounded with frustration and loss of self-esteem can be overwhelming for any child, and such difficulties need to be addressed by an individual who understands these dynamics. This will be discussed in greater detail in Chapters Eight and Twelve.

MEDICAL ASSESSMENT

The third significant member of our team is the physician. This can be a pediatrician or family practitioner with specialized interest and training in the area of attention and learning problems, or perhaps a child psychiatrist or pediatric neurologist also with specialized interest in this area.

Children with attention deficit need a complete physical and neurological exam and may need a neurodevelopmental assessment. The physical examination is performed for the purpose of ruling out any medical problems that could have symptoms like those of attention deficit.

The neurodevelopmental evaluation consists of a series of developmental tasks that have been linked to children with specific learning disabilities as well as to attention deficit. The categories include sequential organization, visual perception, language skills, memory, fine motor coordination, and gross motor ability. An extremely significant part of this evaluation is the selective attention checklist, which rates a child on five aspects of concentration: activity level, distractibility, fatigability, task impersistence, and reflective behavior.

This neurodevelopmental assessment provides a profile of developmental skills and weaknesses. With this information we further define specific learning disabilities as well as attention difficulties.

It should be noted that on the average, most children with attention deficit are neurologically normal and do not need sophisticated neurological work-ups such as EEGs or CAT scans. The vast majority of these test results will be normal and have little or no significance on our overall assessment.

We thus have a three-person perspective for evaluating a child and determining why he or she is having difficulty in school. With these three perspectives, we can separate out the different aspects of attention deficit and understand how they interrelate.

Occasionally, we find that we need a secondary perspective. For example, if, in our evaluation, we find a significant language disability, we may refer that child to a speech and language specialist. If a significant neurological handicapping condition is uncovered, then referral to an appropriate neurologist may also be necessary. These, however, are the exceptions. The vast majority of children will be appropriately diagnosed at this stage so that the correct remediation can take place.

Chapter Twelve will help you locate a clinic that uses a team like the one I have described. It may be that you will have to put together your own team of professionals. Of course, your strategy will depend on the type of resources available in your community, but you can rest assured that there are numerous professionals, organizations, and parents who will be willing to help you.

Important
Background Information

Once you have found professional help and have scheduled an evaluation for your child, you can feel positive that you have taken a significant step toward turning things around. In addition to initiating the diagnostic process, you will also play an important role in the evaluation procedure. It is of utmost importance to the professionals who will evaluate your child to obtain accurate medical, behavioral, and educational histories—essential data can be gleaned from parents and teachers.

You should be asked to fill out questionnaires that detail your child's health and developmental milestones from infancy through the present. Questions regarding your pregnancy—problems; use of medications, cigarettes, alcohol, or drugs; difficulty with delivery; length of pregnancy; and birth weight—top the list. You will be requested to provide information on your child's infancy and development, as well as a history of medical problems. A behavioral inventory indicating both strengths and weaknesses of your child, as well as an educational history outlining specific skills and difficulties, are also essential. An academic history of both parents, as well as the child's siblings, adds further insight into the possibility of a hereditary problem.

Like the data obtained from parents, information gathered from teachers and from school psychologists is extremely valuable. Instructors and counselors are asked to assess the following areas of the student's academic performance: auditory processing (ability to remember oral instruction), oral language, written language, reading, cognition (organization, sequencing, and retention of information), attention (degree of distractibility), activity level, impulsivity, and behavior. Educational personnel are also asked to comment on the child's major difficulties, areas of strength, personality, and habits. Evaluators need to know if the child is frequently absent from school, has repeated grades, or is receiving any special assistance at school. All of this information can be helpful in diagnosing attention deficit problems.

Problems That
Look Like Attention Deficit

When discussing the physical examination segment of the evaluation for attention deficit, I mentioned that there were other problems that should be ruled out. Your child may display many of the symptoms of attention deficit and still have a perfectly normal neurotransmitter metabolism. If that is the case, your child's difficulty in concentrating must be attributed to factors other than attention deficit. There are many problems that can look like a primary attention deficit, and it is important to consider all of the possibilities so that a proper diagnosis can be made. For example, if a child is inattentive due to anxiety or depression, medication will certainly not improve that child's concentration. It is therefore essential to determine whether your child truly has ADD, or whether his attention problems are caused by one or more of the following: anxieties, learning disabilities, medical conditions, or reactions to drugs or other ingested substances. These problems are discussed in greater detail below. The best way to rule out all the imitators of attention deficit is to have your child fully assessed by a team of professionals as outlined in this chapter.

CHRONIC ANXIETY STATES

Perhaps the problem that is most often mistaken for attention deficit is the chronic anxiety state. We all experience times when our thoughts are preoccupied with something other than the situation before us. Our anxiety may be short-term, for example, worry about a dentist appointment this afternoon, or long-term, such as our concern over a relative's deteriorating health.

For children, whose understanding of world events is much narrower, this preoccupation with serious circumstances in their lives can make learning ineffective or sustained attention impossible. These events can include parental separation or divorce, serious illness of a family member, and physical or sexual abuse.

Children dealing with these complex and extremely frightening issues can become depressed and preoccupied. They may also be disorganized, forgetful, inattentive, and somewhat defensive.

As we have seen, several of these characteristics can imitate those of an attention deficit. Unfortunately, the reverse can also be true. A child with an undiagnosed primary form of attention deficit, who has experienced several years of frustration and failure, may take on secondary characteristics of depression. It may be hard to distinguish that child from one who is chronically anxious.

LEARNING DISABILITIES

Learning disabilities form the next major category to examine and distinguish from attention deficit. Basically, a learning disability is a neurological problem that impairs academic achievement. Although concentration difficulties can certainly hinder learning, attention deficit is not generally considered a learning disability. Most professionals view attention deficit as a separate entity, and that will be my approach here. I will frequently refer to learning disabilities, however, for two reasons: 1) Some children with attention deficit have accompanying disabilities. 2) Many resources that are available for learning disabled students also offer assistance for those with attention deficit. (You will read about these resources in Chapters Nine and Twelve).

Since any activity we engage in must provide some reward if we are to continue to pursue it, attention must also be positively reinforced if it is to be sustained. A child who is constantly confused in a particular class will have no reason to struggle to pay attention, and this can be seen in a variety of learning disabilities.

For example, a child may have a receptive language problem. He or she may process auditory material somewhat more slowly than normal. Whenever the instructor is presenting material orally, this child may be chronically lost. It has been measured that a third-grade teacher talks at a rate of approximately 1.5 words per second from a vocabulary of about 5,000 words. A child with a receptive language difficulty may have a processing lag as little as .25 words per second, which could keep him perpetually behind. Since attention is not reinforced, this child may be looking around, drawing pictures in books, disturbing others, etc.

A child with a sequencing problem has a hard time remembering things in order and becomes lost when material is presented in a sequential manner. In preschool, this child has trouble with the days of the week, months of the year, and concepts like "before" and "after." She may ask at age four, "Where are we going yesterday?" When a teacher gives multistepped directions, this child may not understand and may become confused and frustrated. Although the child with a sequencing problem has the ability to concentrate, she may become inattentive because she cannot follow what is going on or know what is expected of her.

So we see, as before, a picture of inattentiveness but, again, not related to ADD and therefore requiring very different kinds of intervention. As a child progresses through school, and more and more material is processed through the auditory pathway with decreasing repetition, we can see this problem becoming more and more debilitating. If a child has a particularly difficult time with sequential material, that child may exhibit characteristics that look a lot like attention deficit.

Attention deficit and dyslexia can also share certain characteristics; for example, dyslexic children are often inattentive and distractible because they have trouble reading and become easily frustrated. They are like those children with receptive language disabilities or sequencing problems, who get "lost" because their attention is not being reinforced. Despite the similarities between some of the characteristics of attention deficit and dyslexia, it is important to understand that these are two distinct problems.

Occasionally in the early grades, other learning disabilities can result in impulsivity and inattentiveness at more discreet times. A child with a dyspraxia, or visual fine motor deficit, may have a very difficult time copying material from the board. The ability to look at something and reproduce it on paper is extremely significant in learning how to write, spell, copy math problems, draw pictures, etc. A visual fine motor deficit can promote feelings of fatigue while the child strains to hold the pencil correctly. Since we do not like to do things that we are not good at, a child with a visual fine motor weakness will attempt to complete tasks rapidly with very little effort and, as a result, may become impulsive and overactive.

It thus becomes imperative to rule out a learning disorder as a primary or secondary cause of attention difficulty. We have begun to see increasing numbers of children with minor learning disabilities. This may in part be related to the increasing sophistication of our neonatal intensive care units. More and more infants who are very premature survive and eventually display minor neurological characteristics which may not be apparent until they enter school. Also, with our increased knowledge and more sophisticated evaluation techniques, many children who were once felt to lack motivation are being found instead to have various types of learning disabilities.

MEDICALLY INDUCED SYMPTOMS

Medically induced symptoms are also essential to distinguish from attention deficit, and, unfortunately, these problems are becoming more widespread. The first one that must be quickly ruled out is any reaction to medications or foods. Several medications exist that can cause many characteristics similar to attention deficit. These can range from medications to treat seizures or asthma to simple over-the-counter medications for the common cold.

Among the common culprits is phenobarbital, which is used to treat seizures and can result in a child being extremely hyperactive and inattentive. About twenty percent of the children who take phenobarbital become fidgety, fussy, whiny, and generally unhappy. A change in behavior becomes readily apparent soon after the child starts taking this medication. If undesirable characteristics are present, a reasonable alternative medication can be found.

The various theophylline preparations commonly used to treat asthma have occasionally led to attention and learning problems, as well as general jitteriness or fidgetiness. Recent research has found that these reactions are not present in the majority of children on these medications. Any behavioral change due to medication should disappear quickly after the medication is discontinued.

Cold preparations with antihistamines, such as Benadryl, can make many children inattentive and chronically drowsy. Certain children can have an unusual reaction to antihistamines and become extremely overactive and inattentive. Decongestants such as pseudophedrine can also hype some children up. Again, all of these reactions effect only a small percentage of children, and most children can take these medications with minimal problems.

Drug abuse can certainly produce side effects that mimic attention deficit. Adolescents using stimulant drugs such as cocaine or "speed" will have many of the attention deficit characteristics. Drug users may appear fidgety and paranoid, constantly looking around and unable to concentrate. Only the adolescent who actually has attention deficit will continue to display these symptoms if he or she stops taking the drugs.

The association between sugar and hyperactivity or attention problems is much more casual than we originally thought. All of us who have seen and evaluated children for attention difficulties have heard sworn testimonial from parents that their already active child turns uncontrollable when he eats a candy bar or drinks a sugary soda. Indeed, sugar can have this effect on a small minority of children. But, unfortunately for all of those nutritionally minded people who would love an easy excuse to discontinue their children's sugar intake, this reaction to sugar is not the norm. Sugar has little if any effect on the majority of children. If, however, your child is one who clearly displays these manifestations, by all means, keep that child off sugar. Again, this represents a very small minority of the children with attention difficulties. Although much has been written about the subject, controlled studies have time and again disproven any positive effect from dietary manipulation. This will be looked at further in the treatment chapter.

OTHER MEDICAL CONDITIONS

Another group of disorders that must be separated out from attention deficit involves other medically related conditions. These can include hearing disorders, which can easily be missed if not looked for. I saw two patients during my fellowship alone who had made it to a major referral center without a hearing screen. In both of these cases, much of their difficulty in school could be attributed to a primary hearing loss.

Other problems must be considered in specific areas of the country. Lead poisoning, for example, must be considered in children who come from older neighborhoods where homes may still have several layers of lead-based paint on the walls. Ingesting paint chips can increase the level of lead in the blood, which mimics the symptoms of primary attention deficit.

Allergic rhinitis, or hay fever, is another medical condition that, if poorly controlled, can certainly simulate an attention problem. When a child's nose is constantly stopped up, he may be unable to breathe adequately. He may appear to be chronically hypoxic (oxygen deficient) and may show signs of irritability, difficulty in concentrating, etc. Once the hay fever is successfully treated, these symptoms disappear.

In areas where allergic rhinitis is a major problem, many children with attention deficit will have the rhinitis problem as well. I have had several patients with classic attention deficit who did not seem to respond to appropriate therapy. Instead of increasing the amount of medication, I looked at the allergy problem and treated both conditions at the same time. This resulted in a total turnaround in these students' attitudes and performance.

Neurological conditions must also be considered in a given child and ruled out. Seizure disorders such as petit mal can cause a child to have a lapse of consciousness for five to ten seconds. During this time the child may stare straight ahead but have none of the abnormal movements that we usually associate with a seizure or convulsion. If a child has these five-to-ten-second lapses frequently throughout the school day, she may have a difficult time keeping her place while reading, following instructions, etc. This will naturally lead to her mind wandering, her not finishing work, and other characteristics that we see in attention deficit. Seizure disorders are rare, but they should be ruled out if the child has had a consistent history of these lapses.

Tourette's Syndrome is another condition that shares many of the characteristics of attention deficit. In fact, attention difficulty is a major part of Tourette's; approximately sixty percent of the Tourette's patients have attention deficit. However, there are many other characteristics that go along with Tourette's Syndrome, including multiple tics, very aggressive lashing-out types of behavior, and unusual sounds and utterances (such as dog and cat noises and foul language). For many years, it was felt that some of the medication used to treat attention problems could lead to Tourette's Syndrome; this recently has been found not to be the case. Although certain of these medications can bring out the characteristics of Tourette's Syndrome, they in no way cause this most uncommon ailment.

PSYCHIATRIC DISORDERS
In addition to the situational anxieties referred to earlier, the more severe psychiatric illnesses can have many of the manifestations of attention deficit. We can see hyperactive, impulsive behavior in certain types of autism, in severe conduct disorders, as well as in pervasive personality disorders. It is not the purpose of this book to go into these disorders, but suffice it to say that children with these psychiatric illnesses may have significant problems relating to other children or to other people in general. If these severe characteristics are present, they certainly need to be investigated by a specialist in the field of child psychiatry.

Unfortunately, in looking at all these great imitators, a special point to keep in mind is that none of these categories is mutually exclusive. Some children with attention problems have associated learning disabilities and situational anxieties. Thus, a doctor is often placed in an unenviable position of resolving the "chicken or the egg" controversy. Is a child inattentive due to a situational anxiety or a receptive language learning disability, or does he have attention deficit with associated problems? For example, an untreated student with attention deficit accompanied by a learning disability may experience failure in school, perpetual criticism, and lack of acceptance by his peers, and these problems will frequently result in anxiety. The distinction of which of these problems comes first is not often easy but is critical for the child.

A Word of Encouragement

As a parent, you can do far more than *anyone* else can to help your child. Professionals may be able to diagnose attention deficit and learning disabilities, prescribe medication when appropriate, or counsel your child, but they do not live with your child and don't provide constant, day-in and day-out support and nurturing. Your love and understanding are of the greatest importance to your child, and, with you as his biggest backer, he has an excellent opportunity to experience success and happiness.

WILLIAM WOODS UNIVERSITY

4.

Attention Deficit
Problems in Preschoolers

Preschool is the logical place to begin if we want to understand attention deficit in children. Let's assume that your preschooler is getting into everything, making one mess after another. He cannot seem to sit still for any type of activity, and he throws screaming fits when he doesn't get his way. Meanwhile, you are beginning to wonder if you will be able to survive the Terrible Twos, Threes, or Fours. What are parents to do?

Considering what you know about attention deficit so far, it is probably hard for you to determine whether your child's behaviors are typical for a child his age or whether his characteristics may indicate attention deficit. So, the purpose of this chapter is to answer the following questions: How do attention deficit preschoolers behave at home, in the classroom, and with their friends? How active is hyperactive? and How do I know if my child has a conduct disorder?

It must be emphasized here that there are many preschool-age children who have attention deficit and are not hyperactive. Such children may be noticeably distractible, impulsive, and disorganized, but these characteristics do not significantly impair their progress during the preschool years and they are rarely brought in for an evaluation at this time.

Although, overall, most children and teens who have attention deficit are *not* hyperactive, I am raising the hyperactivity issue at this point for several important reasons. By far, the majority of the preschoolers who are diagnosed with attention deficit *are* hyperactive, and this is a characteristic that is easy to spot. By discussing the typical behavior of hyperactive children, and by providing some case histories of preschoolers with attention deficit, I hope to show you the difference between hyperactivity and a normal activity level for a young child. This will help you to understand whether your child's activity is average for her age, or whether she is truly hyperactive and is possibly in need of professional evaluation and support.

Likewise, by differentiating between normal preschool behavior and that of the child with a conduct disorder, I will help you to assess your child's behavior patterns. Of course, as I stressed in Chapter Three, it will be impossible for you to make an adequate diagnosis just by reading the material in this book, and I urge you to have your child professionally evaluated.

The Parents' Role

It's important to recognize that parents can have a significant effect on their children's concentration. The degree of attention or behavioral difficulty that a very young child experiences can be related in part to parental handling.

Children with extra-caring and supportive families may receive so much love and understanding that their attention deficit problems will not become apparent as early as they would under other, less desirable circumstances. In addition, these children often are given needed freedom and space to explore, and this helps in controlling their impulsive styles, which are not as much of a problem as they would be in a stricter, more confining environment.

I recently diagnosed a seven-year-old whose mother has had extensive psychological training in working with attention deficit children. The boy was extremely active as a preschooler, and I am firmly convinced that effective parenting served to delay the discovery of his attention difficulties. The parents did an excellent job of handling this child and practicing positive behavioral management techniques. If the parents had been less knowledge-able, the child's attention deficit symptoms might have surfaced much sooner, requiring help for him at age three or four, rather than at age seven.

However, although the parents' role can certainly affect behaviors, it is important to remember that the characteristics of attention problems are inherent and would be there despite the style of parenting. Attention deficit, as we have seen, is a neurophysiological condition. It is not brought on by poor parenting. The child with preschool attention deficit symptoms, even in the best of environments, will still display some of these characteristics.

As I have stated, there are many conditions at all ages that can imitate attention deficit, and it's essential to adequately evaluate a child and separate these out. With the preschool-age child, this can be quite challenging due to the lack of cognitive development. The family assessment is crucial: a look at parent-child interaction can be most revealing.

The Hyperactive Preschooler

We are going to explore two types of attention deficit in preschoolers. The first of these is the classic case of attention deficit with hyperactivity (and without any significant conduct disorder). Children of this type seem pretty normal as infants. They are not often noted to be excessively colicky or to have a disproportionate number of feeding difficulties; these children can be very cuddly, happy babies. It is not until they approach the toddler stage that they begin to display some mood fluctuations and temper tantrums. These outbursts are often, but not always, a bit excessive when compared to the usual mood alterations of two- or three-year-olds.

Children who have attention deficit with hyperactivity (ADDH) usually have difficulty pursuing the typical toddler activities for any length of time. These children may have a tornadic effect on a room, pulling all the toys off the shelves, dumping out baskets of cars, and knocking over blocks. If an object has not been totally secured to the ground, it will be picked up or pushed over. It is also at this stage that there is the first indication that these children's ability to focus and concentrate is somewhat impaired. They may watch television for five minutes, get distracted, and color for five minutes. Then they may notice a friend playing outside and want to run out and hop on a riding toy, even though it is eight in the evening and bath time. It also must be mentioned that a high activity level is always more accentuated within a group. One-to-one, many of these children can settle down and, with guidance, pursue an activity a bit longer. However, a lack of sustained attention, even one-to-one, usually becomes readily apparent with children who have attention problems.

It is also interesting to note that sometimes, even in a group, hyperactive children (like older individuals with attention deficit) will focus in on an activity by blocking out the rest of the world. Then, they may concentrate for what seems like an abnormally long time on watching a television program, digging in the sand, looking at a book, or whatever. When a child's focus is locked on an activity, it may be extremely hard to distract her. You may need to go to the child and touch her shoulder in order to get her attention.

Parents and other individuals who deal with children who have attention deficit need to understand that, when these children do manage to focus on something, they really don't see or hear what is going on around them. It is frustrating to try to work with a child when you think that child is ignoring you. But we need to remember that the child with attention deficit has to tune everything else out in order to concentrate. That child probably isn't hearing you and ignoring you; she probably doesn't hear you at all. The child may not have this tuning out ability all the time, and it is rare for a child to accomplish this kind of focus in a group setting. It is important for adults who work with these children to recognize this "blocking out" process and treat the children with understanding.

In a preschool classroom, hyperactive children may encounter more frustration than they do at home. These children may have little or no interest in blocks except in a very hurried or haphazard approach. Their main interest may be in knocking down the block buildings that other children have painstakingly erected—such actions are rarely popular with peers or with teachers. Hyperactive children may find it very difficult to sit still through an entire story, song, or game. These children move rapidly from one toy or activity to another, not slowing down to play for a significant amount of time with anything.

If hyperactive children are not accustomed to sharing, they may become terribly disappointed or annoyed when they come back to a toy and find that another child has it. "I had it first," carries little weight with the preschool teacher in this situation. Sharing can be a very hard lesson for any toddler, and it seems especially difficult for the hyperactive child.

Hyperactive children are also very impulsive. They are so active and move so rapidly that they never stop to consider the consequences of their actions. These children leap before they look, displaying no caution, and it doesn't occur to them that they might get hurt.

Unfortunately, hyperactive children are frequent visitors to the pediatrician's office with concussions, lacerations, fractured collar bones, and bruised elbows. They are forever getting hurt but never learning from the experience. They don't know why they jump out of trees; it just seems to be a good idea at the time. A five-year-old whose mom was concerned when he rode downhill on his bike standing on the seat on one foot insisted, "I'm big. I can do anything I want without getting hurt." Regrettably, it doesn't always work that way. It's not that these hyperactive children enjoy misbehaving, and they aren't trying to test anyone; they just go for what they want at that moment—fearlessly!

At times, however, these children do slow down enough to interact, and we find that they can be very loving, caring individuals. They want very much to please, and have a hard time understanding why everyone is so frustrated with them. When, in the relentless pursuit of their activity, they do break something or hit someone, they may truly feel remorse. They fail to learn from these experiences, though, and, as the acts of aggression increase, these children begin to alienate their peers and preschool instructors.

It is so important for the adults who deal with these children to understand them and to try to be patient with them. Of course, this is easier said than done, but a patient, loving, and firm approach can be very effective with hyperactive preschoolers. These children need a lot of guidance and supervision. They also need consistency, and above all they need love.

Of course, all children need these supports. But, children who have attention deficit with hyperactivity may receive less backup in the long run, because adults may experience a great deal of frustration when working with them. When children feel unloved or think that everyone is mad at them, their self-esteem suffers greatly. You don't want your child's self-esteem to diminish; you don't want her to think that she's "bad" or that everyone hates her. So your extra reserve of patience will be called upon.

The following case will enable you to see how these traits are actually displayed in the behavior of a child, so let me introduce you to Randy.

RANDY

Randy is a perfect example of the hyperactive child with attention deficit. He was referred to me at the age of five, due to his high activity level, restlessness, and distractibility. Randy was progressing at either an average or above-average level in all academic areas, but he needed direct one-to-one input to complete any task. He was so easily distracted by any noise or activity that his instructor expressed serious reservations as to whether he could ever remain focused long enough to effectively complete first-grade work.

In reviewing Randy's medical history, I found nothing out of the ordinary. Randy was the product of a full-term pregnancy with a normal delivery four days prior to the expected due date. He weighed six pounds, fourteen ounces at birth and experienced no problems during his nursery stay, leaving the hospital with his mother. Randy had no major illnesses in the infancy period, and experienced no feeding or sleeping problems during the first year of life.

Developmental milestones, such as crawling, walking, and talking, were also felt to be within a normal time frame. Randy crawled at six months, walked at ten months, and spoke his first words prior to one year of age.

Randy's attention problems began long before kindergarten, however. His preschool teacher had noted that he had problems due to a high activity level and "rowdy" behavior. Although he had progressed at an average rate academically, Randy was observed to be extremely restless and distractible in class.

At home, Randy was also noted to be very active, needing firm directions continually to complete any task. He had a difficult time sitting through a meal, could watch television for only short periods of time, and was very athletic and active most of the time.

Randy was cared for by both of his parents, who had done a good job of coping with him but were starting to show a few signs of stress. They wanted Randy to settle down some, at home as well as at school, and he just didn't seem capable of slowing himself. They had to watch him carefully, because his impulsivity sometimes put him in dangerous situations. He couldn't seem to think before acting, and he had, on several occasions, dashed in front of another kid on a swing or chased a ball into the street without looking, and Randy's parents were concerned about his safety.

Among his peers, Randy was very outspoken and tended to be a leader. He had many friends his own age and played well with both older and younger children. However, when engaged in play, Randy usually liked to be in control. He was generally well liked and was a very happy and loving child.

This child clearly displayed characteristics of attention deficit with hyperactivity and with no accompanying conduct disorder. He was distractible, impulsive, poorly organized, and needed constant one-to-one direction to sustain his attention. In addition, Randy was extremely active, often appearing to move in many directions at the same time. Despite this, he was sensitive, loving, and wanted very much to be able to pursue meaningful interactions. However, to accomplish this, Randy needed appropriate intervention in order to curb his activity and restlessness and enable him to concentrate in class. This can be accomplished in a variety of ways, as I will outline in Chapter Ten. If Randy's attention deficit had remained undiagnosed, his behavior would inevitably have become more and more alienating, and would have resulted in greater frustration on Randy's part.

Randy's case shows us that many kids with attention deficit can be loving, caring individuals who may test every rule to the limit. It is helpful for parents and teachers to understand why these children act the way they do and have the problems that they have. This understanding, combined with the practice of many of the behavioral modification and classroom management techniques that I will discuss later in this book, will enable adults to work more effectively with children who have attention deficit.

The Hyperactive Child with a Conduct Disorder

The other type of attention deficit seen in preschoolers is also a hyperactivity variant, but with an accompanying conduct disorder as well. Individuals with this form of attention deficit commonly stand out from early on, usually before the hyperactive children described above. The children who seem to have an accompanying conduct disorder have cycles that are often irregular from the beginning. They seem to have a hard time falling into any routine eating or sleeping pattern, often awaking at different times, with length of naps and sleep cycles varying. Their crying patterns are frequently intense and will not stop when their diapers are changed or after eating.

These children have a very difficult time adapting to change. Normal transitional activities are always traumatic for them. They will reject cereal initially, cry when approached by strangers, startle easily with sudden noises, and cry immediately when awakened. Hyperactive infants with conduct disorders tend to be more colicky than other babies. Their colic can persist longer than the usual infant crying periods.

As these children progress, this increased intensity and difficulty with satisfaction extends into the development of all new milestones. As noted, they often cry when new foods are introduced and tend to be very picky. During physical examinations or temperature checks, these children kick and scream continually. They often cry when toys are taken away and are much more difficult to distract from one activity to another than other children. These children frequently lose interest in new toys very quickly and will cry immediately if left alone, even briefly.

Hygiene at this stage is also rejected. Toddlers with conduct disorders often hate having their faces or hands washed. A haircut is even more likely to be hair-raising.

Accompanying such activities, these preschoolers begin to experience their first temper tantrums, which are usually earlier, longer, more persistent, and more frequent than the usual "Terrible Two" temper outbursts. What is even more upsetting is the lashing out that we often see in these tantrums. These children appear so obsessed with anger and frustration that they will lash out at anyone in their path, including their parents or day-care instructors. This is exceedingly frustrating for the parents, since there is little if any way to console such children until their tantrums are complete.

This is also the first indication of the socialization difficulties that these children encounter. Social problems will compound the frustrations that these preschoolers are experiencing in other areas. Children with attention deficit and conduct disorders are often very aggressive and want to be in total control in peer interactions. When they don't get their way, they frequently become aggressive. They alienate other children, as well as the other children's parents—many parents will prefer that their children not socialize with someone so temperamental and pushy. The parents may even worry that this child will harm their child or their property. A distraught mother once confided to me that no one had shown up for her hyperactive son's fourth birthday party. She and her husband had to hurriedly recruit some younger neighborhood children to help their son celebrate.

At home, the children with conduct disorders continue to have difficulty fitting into family socialization activities. They have trouble sitting through a meal, eat quickly and prefer snacks and junk food to meals. Time and frequency of bowel movements can vary, and these children may suffer from chronic constipation or soiling.

The matter of discipline is extremely frustrating for parents and preschool instructors alike, since punishment seems to have little significance for these children. Such preschoolers respond poorly to any type of physical punishment, which often has the undesirable result of creating more resistance. This, incidentally, places these children at a high risk for abuse and neglect, due to the tremendous level of frustration they create in their caretakers.

Because the tremendous patience and mutual support of both parents is so essential, anything other than the most supportive of families can be literally torn apart by these children. If this happens, the deterioration of the family will of course serve to perpetuate the alienation and frustration of the hyperactive child.

Due to the extensive needs of such children and their families, it is essential that these parents and their physicians together mobilize all community resources available while the child is still very young. All adults dealing with these children need to bolster each other and provide the appropriate environmental constraints and supports necessary to alleviate some of the tremendous sense of frustration these children encounter.

Whether these children should be classified as conduct disorders first or whether they are truly a conduct disorder variant of attention deficit is far from decided. Indeed, many could represent a more pervasive personality disorder as well. Fortunately, these are clearly a minority of the attention deficit children I see, and the treatment for these children is quite different from that used for patients with less severe attention difficulties.

The following case history outlines the characteristics I have described above.

SUSIE

Four-year-old Susie was referred to me with a history of hyperactivity, insatiability, and violent temper tantrums. The first time I saw Susie, she had just ripped the paper sheet off the examining room's cot, torn the blood pressure cups off the wall, tossed the books and magazines on the floor, and turned over the trash-can. She was also screaming at her parents, because they wouldn't let her climb on the toy shelves.

Susie's parents desperately wanted help. The mother was an elementary school counselor who knew a lot about behavior management but found Susie difficult to control. Her husband, an architect, was equally frustrated by his daughter's behavior. They had an older son who had never posed any problems, and then along had come Susie.

It is important to look at Susie's past history. She weighed six pounds, seven ounces at birth (a full-term, emergency Caesarean-section delivery due to placenta praevia). Susie did well in the hospital and went home with her mother after three days. Developmental milestones were well within normal limits, including crawling at six months, sitting up at seven months, walking at ten months, and using single words at eleven and twelve months of age.

As an infant, Susie was very highstrung. She cried intensely when she was hungry or wet, and was hard to console.

When Susie reached the toddler stage, she became extremely active and was often destructive. She charged into things impulsively and was frequently injured. She was also very aggressive around other children.

When Susie focused on a particular desire, she would scream uncontrollably until that desire was satisfied. During those times, it was almost impossible to distract her from that pursuit. Her satisfaction with a coveted object or activity lasted only until she became obsessed with something else, and then she would repeat the behavior. It was almost impossible to take Susie to a grocery store or a shopping mall without this type of incident taking place.

Susie had significant mood swings and violent temper outbursts, sometimes crying uncontrollably for as long as an hour. Not a particularly affectionate child, she had trouble relating to others, and it was hard for even her parents to relate to her. Bonding with this child seemed impossible.

As she got older, Susie's problems intensified. She became even more impulsive and insatiable, and her parents could do nothing to change her behavior. They enrolled her in preschool, hoping that would help, but the teacher couldn't handle her either. Susie constantly posed a threat to the other children in her class—as well as to herself.

When I evaluated Susie I found that she indeed had attention deficit with hyperactivity and an accompanying conduct disorder. I prescribed a stimulant medication for her, and the results brought hope to her distraught parents. The medication controlled Susie's hyperactivity and improved her symptoms of impulsivity and moodiness. By working together to enforce a strict behavior modification program and to avoid potential hazards (such as trips to the mall), Susie's parents were able to bring some order and happiness into their home life.

Summary

These two preschool presentations illustrate very different degrees of similar problems, and the remediation and treatment are equally different. Where a particular child falls on this continuum and how the various forms of treatment are initiated is still a very fascinating and often frustrating problem for physicians and mental health personnel. As noted, these children do not respond as universally positively as do older children with attention deficit; preschoolers need an individual therapeutic approach.

There have been several statistical studies that have pointed out significant variables at birth when you compare a hyperactive child with conduct disorder to children who do not have attention deficit. Researchers have looked at findings regarding maternal health and age, as well as the child's health during infancy and the child's coordination. These studies have indicated that mothers of hyperactive children do tend to be younger and experience poorer health during pregnancy than do mothers of normal children or even children with attention deficit who are not hyperactive. Another indication is that health problems during infancy and poor coordination are also more prevalent among hyperactive children.

However, many hyperactive children have none of these risk factors, coming from healthy, well-adjusted families with normal pregnancy histories. I find that many of the mothers with conduct disorder children report normal pregnancies.

Prior to evaluating children, we do ask the parents for a complete medical history, including pertinent information regarding the pregnancy. We look for the variables mentioned above, but do not base a diagnosis upon this information by any means. Mothers should not blame themselves for their children's attention deficit, feeling guilt about their young age, toxemia, or other factors regarding the pregnancy. As we have seen, attention deficit is usually a genetic problem and is unrelated to maternal age and health.

We can thus see that attention deficit in preschoolers involves two distinct variants. Both have the classical characteristics of attention deficit with hyperactivity; however, the children with the significant conduct disorder associated with attention deficit seem to be at a far greater risk as far as prognosis for successful treatment. I will look at the different methods used for both of these groups in my discussion of medical treatment in Chapter Seven.

5.

Attention Deficit Problems in Early Elementary School

The children in this age group who are beginning to experience academic difficulties are most responsive to treatment. Careful testing must be completed to determine the actual cause of the learning problems. If your child is correctly diagnosed with attention deficit, and is appropriately treated, there will probably be a noted improvement in his or her ability to achieve in school.

Of course, not all children will be as fortunate as your child. But a problem must be acknowledged before it can be overcome, and many of the children in early elementary school who have attention deficit will not be diagnosed. Although sixty percent of the students I evaluate are in this age group, there are large numbers of children with attention deficit who are never referred for testing. Instead, they are given labels such as "underachieving," "lazy," "unmotivated," and "uncaring." As they progress through school, their learning problems may multiply and their self-esteem hit rock-bottom. Therefore, identifying the problem and beginning treatment before the child gets older may be crucial.

Why Are These Kids
Hard to Spot?

Children who first display concentration problems in the early elementary grades can be quite difficult to pick out and are frequently misunderstood. In contrast, unlike the hyperactive preschoolers discussed in Chapter Four, who are not at all hard to spot, but are most difficult to treat, the early elementary-age students can be hard to recognize, but, once diagnosed, respond well to treatment. The difference is that the preschool-age children who are diagnosed with attention deficit are almost always hyperactive. As we have seen, hyperactive children are anything but subtle.

There will always be a few hyperactive children who will reach elementary school or maybe even junior high without being diagnosed. Frequently, these students are males whose pediatricians refer to them as "all boy" when asked by parents if these children are hyperactive. Recently I evaluated a fourth-grade male who had attention deficit difficulties with hyperactivity. Philip had been extremely active and difficult from birth, and his teachers commented on his high activity level. The parents had repeatedly questioned the child's doctor and had been reassured that their son was simply "a typical little boy." By the time Philip was brought to me for testing, he was ten years old. His reading was on a second grade level, and his math skills on a third grade level. He responded well to medication and to resource assistance available at his school. Philip is now in fifth grade, doing fifth-grade-level math and fourth-grade reading.

However, most early elementary school children with attention deficit, unlike Philip, are neither hyperactive nor aggressive. They have "classical attention deficit," without hyperactivity, and are not perpetually out of their seats, running down the hall, or directly in the middle of disturbances. They usually are able to sit at their desks, and they appear to be listening to the teacher. An untrained observer of such students would probably conclude that they are not bothering others, and, thus, could not possibly have an attention problem. This can often be far from the truth and, therefore, it is absolutely essential that these children be adequately evaluated before a diagnosis or treatment is arrived at.

Another reason for the necessity of a formal assessment is that children can be subject to many competing influences. They can display characteristic symptoms of attention deficit that, as we have seen, may stem from various learning disabilities or psychological problems. We will examine these difficulties in greater detail later in this chapter. At this point, I just want to reiterate that it is extremely important to rule out these other possible problems and avoid inappropriate treatment for these children. A misdiagnosis may indeed leave permanent psychological scars, and those scars, in the long run, can be very debilitating. With that in mind, let us look carefully at the early elementary-school-age children—a very exciting and rewarding group of children to care for.

Characteristics of This Age Group

Most early elementary-school-age children with attention deficit are diagnosed in the first or second grade, but occasionally some of these children are spotted in kindergarten, as well. Many children with attention deficit appear quite bright and display no severe behavioral problems. More typically, they just don't seem to be able to concentrate sufficiently to understand what is happening in class.

It is quite common to hear from concerned parents that these children do fine when they work with them one-to-one. However, in the midst of a classroom, such students seem to be a thousand miles away. Another common observation is that these children can spell one hundred percent of their spelling words the night before the test, but at exam time they act as though they have never seen the words.

This is exceedingly frustrating for parents and teachers, who know that these children are not achieving their full potential. You have probably talked with them over and over again about doing their best in school. They say with sincerity that they want to do their best, but their schoolwork doesn't improve. Often these children with attention deficit are doing their best. For some

reason, though, they can't seem to put it all together in the classroom. Many of these children end up being labeled (as I mentioned earlier) and being blamed for problems that are not within
their control, as well as being even more frustrated than the adults
who work with them.

It is not uncommon for many of these students to be retained in
kindergarten or first grade in the hope that one additional year of
maturity will really make the difference and they will proceed to
do quite well. Unfortunately, this is rarely the case.

DISTRACTIBILITY

These children display the classic symptomatology that we have
referred to as attention deficit without hyperactivity. As noted,
one-to-one and without outside distraction, they can often concentrate and learn quite adequately. On the other hand, in a busy
classroom it may be absolutely impossible for these students to
sustain their attention. They will be listening to the teacher one
minute, and then someone will sneeze or drop a book, causing
their attention to be lost, and they often may not be able to redirect
themselves to the original focus.

Their distractibility also makes it exceedingly hard for these
children to complete an assignment. They will start out with a
strong effort, but they will soon lose their train of thought and
begin to focus on another activity. They may not even get past
putting a heading on the paper, before they completely forget all
about the assigned task and start thinking about something else.

Last week a patient's mother related a classic example of
distractibility. Her seven-year-old son is in the junior football
league, and since he is one of the smallest and youngest children
he does not get to play very often. Rather than sitting with the
team, watching the game, and trying to pick up pointers, he is off
chasing butterflies, getting drinks, and playing his own fantasy
football games on the sidelines. He is totally unaware of what the
other children are doing, but just happy to be on the team and be
at the game. This child usually has no idea who is winning or that
other people in the crowd may be watching him with amusement.

On a positive side, the child does not feel badly about not

playing. In fact, it is only when the coach calls his name or looks for him because he is not where he should be that the child even perceives this to be a problem. Although at age seven, this boy has difficulty concentrating in the classroom, his attention deficit may not have as much of a detrimental effect on his sports or his social activities. However, he will be at risk later on when socially unacceptable behavior and alienation from his peers may become more pronounced.

FREE FLIGHT OF IDEAS
Related to these children's distractibility is their free flight of ideas. This characteristic can be troublesome for individuals of all ages, but the child in elementary school is particularly bothered by this trait, which causes him or her to daydream and to miss important facts or concepts that are being taught.

Let's look at an example. Suppose that the teacher is talking about the upcoming presidential election. Six-year-old Amanda starts to think about George Washington and the cherry tree. The child is then reminded of the cherry tree in her own front yard. Amanda raises her hand, and, when called upon, remarks, "The tree in our front yard has pretty yellow leaves on it." Amanda has not been listening to the teacher at all and has no idea who the two presidential candidates are.

Free flight of ideas is a constant problem for young school children with attention deficit. Their minds may wander so extensively that they may actually spend a large portion of their schoolday in a world of imagination. While they think about birthday parties, baseball games, vacations, or whatever else happens to cross their minds, they may look like they are paying very close attention to the teacher, and, in most instances, the teacher receives no indication that these students are daydreaming.

IMPULSIVITY
Nonhyperactive children with attention deficit in early elementary school show many of the other characteristics of hyperactive children, but not to the same degree. For example, the children without hyperactivity may be very impulsive, but their impulsivity

is under better control and does not surface until they are in a more chaotic environment.

Impulsivity can seriously affect schoolwork. An impulsive child may not take the time to think through what he is doing in regard to a written assignment. He may work quickly and carelessly, making frequent spelling errors by leaving out or reversing the order of letters. The child may make many mistakes on simple math problems due to putting numbers in the wrong columns or using an incorrect procedure, such as subtracting instead of adding.

SOCIAL IMMATURITY

Likewise, the nonhyperactive children with attention deficit are certainly more socially immature than children without attention problems, but not to the extent that they quickly alienate all their peers. For example, a child with ADDH may be so socially immature that she really has no recognition of social cues and will often burst out with one faux pas after another, resulting in very few sustained friendships. The child with attention deficit without hyperactivity, on the other hand, often does have many friends. This child may simply be unaware of many subtle nuances and may experience some social problems as she progresses through elementary school.

A perfect illustration is found in the case study of an eight-year-old boy who wanted desperately to be popular. He decided to invite all the other boys in his neighborhood to a party. As he handed out the invitations, he hugged all the boys—the result was that he did not get the reaction he wanted.

We do not want to change these children into social conformists—on the contrary—but we do want them to be able to develop their own social sophistication, so they will be able to recognize what is acceptable and what's not. Hopefully, as these children mature, they will be able to use their aggressive, outgoing nature to their advantage in dealing with the adult world.

DISORGANIZATION

The other characteristic of attention deficit that is very common in these children is a lack of organization. This is usually frustrating to the parents, who go to great lengths to organize their child's day. Inevitably, the child will bring home the wrong book, forget the dentist appointment she was told to come home for right after school, or fail to turn in the homework that she spent an hour completing painstakingly with her parents the night before.

Such children seem to have an extremely difficult time balancing all of the responsibilities placed upon them, so they therefore find it difficult to develop some structure in their lives. Again, their lives are not disordered to the degree that they never seem to know what is going on. It is just that these children rarely complete what they start or get to the right place at the right time.

This, of course, applies to chores at home as well. Children with attention deficit fully intend to cut the lawn. It is only that they get somewhat distracted by the neighborhood football game and just forget to go back to finish—leaving the lawn mower, rake, and broom right in the middle of the yard. The lawn somehow never seems to get cut, or at least not completed, despite their admirable intentions.

These children may also be very forgetful when it comes to their belongings. They may continually misplace things, such as articles of clothing, shoes, toys, or books. Unless the parents are extremely organized themselves, they may have a nightmarish time getting the child off to school on time with matching shoes and/or socks, jacket, lunch box, textbooks, and homework. The child will have no idea where the missing items are. Homework may eventually turn up under the child's bed, and a lost lunch box may be found full of toys in the bottom of the clothes hamper.

More often than not, the child with attention deficit will have a disorganized bedroom and a messy desk at school. The child probably doesn't care how his bedroom or desk appears, but may feel somewhat frustrated when he can't find things. Some children with attention deficit may actually prefer to have their rooms "trashed out." They may say that it is easier for them to find their belongings when these items are spread out all over the floor. If you go in and pick up your child's room, he truly may be upset that his clothes and books aren't all over the floor where he left them.

The child who has attention deficit may also have an unkempt appearance. Buttons, snaps, and zippers may not be fastened properly, hair may not get a great deal of care, and shirts may clash with pants—assuming, of course, that the parents are not highly involved in the child's grooming.

There is also the perception that many of these children are constantly testing adults. They have also, out of frustration, been known to have significant temper tantrums, but this behavior is usually much more indicative of the hyperactive children described in the previous chapter.

Early elementary-age children with attention deficit are usually very affectionate and often very social children, which makes the diagnosis of ADD quite surprising to many of their parents and educators. Many adults still equate attention deficit with hyperactivity, which would mean that nonhyperactive students wouldn't even be considered for the diagnosis.

These children who are not hyperactive are not easy to diagnose, even for a trained observer, who usually will see them one-to-one. It is only when they are in a group, where they need to pay attention, that the characteristics become much more readily apparent.

In fact, many of the attention deficit characteristics sound like normal childhood traits. Most children are distractible, forgetful, impulsive, and moody at times. We all daydream occasionally and have trouble concentrating on reading material or the words of a speaker. So, what makes individuals with attention deficit different from others who experience similar problems? As I mentioned earlier, it is the severity and persistence of the attention difficulty, as well as the child's inability to function in school according to his intellectual potential, that distinguishes the child who has attention deficit.

Problems That Mimic
Attention Deficit in This Age Group

Understanding the subtleties of this group and the excellent response these children usually have to medication, it would be worthwhile to further explore the characteristics and problems that may simulate attention deficit and need to be ruled out. As we saw in Chapter Three, there are many difficulties that can masquerade as attention difficulties, and some are particularly applicable to early school-age children.

AUDITORY AND LANGUAGE PROBLEMS

Auditory and language problems can include auditory perceptual disabilities or receptive language problems. Some children may have a difficult time distinguishing subtle differences in the sounds of words, making it very difficult for them to follow a conversation. Since many of the words in a sentence may not fit together to turn into a meaningful thought, attention is very difficult to reinforce.

Other children with auditory problems may process speech correctly, but more slowly. Thus they are chronically behind in following what the instructor is saying and have a lot of trouble comprehending classroom discussions and explanations. If you speak slowly for these children, they can easily follow what is being said.

Since both types of auditory difficulties will lead to chronic inattention, children with these problems will be easily distracted in class but will do quite well in one-to-one interactions.

FINE MOTOR DIFFICULTIES

Young children who are unable to control pencils, crayons, or scissors are at a definite disadvantage in elementary school. They perform tasks requiring fine motor skills much more slowly than the other children and often lag behind in getting their work done. As more written work is required of them, they may become quite frustrated and lose interest in their schoolwork. At this point, they may start daydreaming or misbehaving in class.

VISUAL PERCEPTUAL PROBLEMS

Many children may also have visual perceptual problems where they will reverse letters such as *b* and *d* or occasionally whole words, such as *was* and *saw*. This information is somehow coded backwards, and will certainly be evidenced in many visual fine motor tasks, such as copying from the blackboard, drawing, or spelling. Visual perceptual problems can also affect reading, since the students may skip certain sentences or words and thus have trouble following from one line to the next. Students who frequently lose their place when reading may find it very difficult to concentrate and stay on task.

SEQUENCING DISABILITIES

Poor sequencing skills can also frustrate a child and lead to inattention and distractibility. Sequencing skills enable us to get things or ideas in the right order and to blend parts into a whole. A child with a sequencing difficulty may have trouble developing phonetic skills in the early grades and cannot possibly follow multistep directions. She may seem chronically lost when the rest of the class is working on the second part of a three-part assignment since she doesn't know what comes after part one. She also may become confused with the particular steps in problems, which can be disastrous in trying to master mathematical calculations. Again we see that attention and concentration are lost.

POOR MEMORY SKILLS

Another learning disability that can look like attention deficit in the early elementary-age child is a memory problem with an inability to record and integrate material that is being presented. Memory skills are divided between long-term and short-term memory. Short-term memory may be represented by a child who can learn his spelling words perfectly the night before a test. If the words are not committed to long-term memory, the child may still miss fifty percent on his spelling test the next day. We have seen that this problem can also be related to an attention or focusing problem as well. Indeed, the child lacking in memory skill may need to go over information many times in order to master long-term memory.

Making a Diagnosis

As one can see, a differential diagnosis for this age child is critical and needs to be clearly defined before any treatment should be provided. To complicate this even further is the fact that many of these children with attention deficit will have one or two of these learning disabilities as well. It is thus imperative that these children get full and complete evaluations that diagnose these problems and thus provide appropriate treatment. The accompanying learning difficulties are often more minor than the attention deficit. When attention deficit is properly diagnosed and treated, the child may then be able to compensate for other mild disabilities.

All of us have a series of strengths and weaknesses that, as students, we compensate for and work around. There are no perfect brains and we all must use our strengths to minimize the weaknesses in our learning styles. It may be only when we have several of these problems together, such as two or three specific learning disabilities, or possibly a learning disability and an attention problem, that a particular weakness becomes relevant. Thus, by curing the attention problem, the one area of learning disability often can be easily overcome, and not be a particular problem for that child later on. It is only with the accompanied attention problem that it becomes overwhelming and much more problematic.

Psychological Factors

The other essential ingredient that one must begin to consider when dealing with this age group will be discussed more thoroughly in subsequent chapters. I am referring to a psychological or family difficulty. As we will see, many children with attention deficit will become somewhat depressed, which tends to perpetuate their problems. On the other hand, a child who is in a family that is going through an angry divorce, or a child who has been physically or sexually abused, may be chronically anxious, making it hard for the child to concentrate. This chronic anxiety may indeed not be picked up until a child is forced to pay attention in class. Again, this makes the appropriate evaluation essential.

With these ideas in mind, let us look at a typical profile of an early elementary-age child with attention deficit. We must remember that these children are impulsive when compared to a normal child, but not nearly to the degree of a child with hyperactivity. They are inattentive, insatiable, socially immature, and distractible, but much more so in a large group than on their own. These problems tend to increase as the children advance in school and become more frustrated and alienated.

ROB

Rob is an eight-year-old male who was referred to my evaluation center with a history of an inability to complete his work and failure to progress in his early reading and spelling skills, despite persistent attempts by his parents to assist him.

A study of Rob's medical history reveals that he was the product of a full-term pregnancy with no complications. He was breast-fed for the first six months of life and was noted to have no feeding or sleeping difficulties in infancy. Developmental milestones were all consistent for his age, and Rob was noted to be a generally cuddly, happy baby.

His family history indicates that Rob was the first child born to a twenty-one-year-old mother and a twenty-year-old father, both of whom were college drop-outs. When Rob was eighteen months old, his mother returned to school to obtain a teaching certificate. She had her second child, a daughter, several years later, and is now teaching elementary school.

The father, who had finished only one year of junior college before dropping out to get married, was working as a mechanic at the time of Rob's birth. Since then, the father has changed jobs several times and has taken some technical courses. He is currently employed as an electronics technician.

Rob's academic history dates back to the time when his mother returned to college and placed him in day care. He did well, but was noted to be aggressive at times. When Rob was three years old, his parents enrolled him in preschool, and his teachers reported that Rob had difficulty staying in his seat and occasionally disturbed other children, but was not a serious behavioral problem.

Rob's mother admitted upon reflection (and now comparing Rob's behavior to that of her three-year-old daughter) that Rob usually liked to be on the go from one activity to the next. She had always related this characteristic to his just being "all boy."

When Rob started kindergarten, he had just turned five and was one of the youngest children in class. He was noted to be somewhat socially immature, with frequent baby talk and a disorganized approach to his work. It should be mentioned, however, that he was very well liked by his teacher and peers. Due to his immaturity and young age, the teacher and parents decided that Rob should be retained in kindergarten.

After a second year, Rob was placed in the first grade, where his problems compounded. He had a very difficult time completing his work and was easily distracted by the slightest disturbance in the classroom. He immediately fell behind in his early reading and spelling skills. Rob's mother at first attempted to help him, which was frustrating for her, so she hired a tutor who worked with Rob one hour a day after school. This was helpful, and Rob was able to pass into the second grade. However, he began to develop a disdain for school and did not want to go. During the summer between first and second grade, Rob was tested and found to have an overall IQ of 114; however, his achievement levels were all in the low to middle first grade.

The first two months of the second grade were very frustrating for Rob and his parents. He began forgetting to bring his books home and would forget to turn in the homework that his parents spent the evening before completing with him. It was at this time that Rob was referred to my evaluation center by a school psychologist.

Since he had recently received an academic evaluation, Rob underwent psychological and neurodevelopmental testing at my clinic. The psychological evaluation displayed a very likeable eight-year-old male who was beginning to feel inadequate toward his academic abilities and frustrated by his apparent difficulty there. He still generally felt secure in his relationship with his parents and received a lot of positive self-esteem from being a star on the soccer team. However, he was clearly showing a great deal of anxiety in relationship to school.

In the neurodevelopmental assessment, there were two significant findings. First, Rob displayed some noted difficulty in sequential organizational tasks; second, on a scale throughout the
neurodevelopmental exam rating Rob on impulsivity, distractibility, attention to detail, and performance and consistency, Rob
was clearly two standard deviations below the mean, indicating a
probable primary attention deficit. He was thus treated for these
two problems and proceeded to have a complete turnaround in
his academic performance. After six months of treatment, Rob
was placed in the high math group and was generally achieving at
the upper end of his class by the end of the second grade.

In presenting Rob's case, I included a complete history in order
to illustrate several characteristics that make this a typical example of attention deficit without hyperactivity. First, a family history
reveals the behavior of Rob's father, which is not atypical in
parents of children with attention deficit. The history of moving
from job to job or even from spouse to spouse is a familiar one.
Next, Rob began to have some trouble during early preschool, but
it wasn't excessive and was never felt to be a major problem. Once
he did reach elementary school and was required to sustain his
attention to a far greater degree, organize his work, and complete
assignments, the real difficulties began.

Rob, being a very likeable child, received a lot of support from
his parents and teachers; however, after several years, it became
clear that this was not going to solve the problem and indeed
there seemed to be something significant that was getting in Rob's
way. Thus, in treating Rob's attention problem and paying attention to his sequential organizational difficulty, we were able to
turn this around, rebuild his confidence in school, and begin him
on what will hopefully be a very successful school career.

This case history illustrates some of the classic characteristics
we see when early elementary-age children display symptoms of
attention deficit. In Chapter Seven, we will go over the specifics
of treatment for assisting these children in overcoming their difficulties.

6.

Attention Deficit Problems
in Junior High or High School

If you have a teenage child who is having trouble in school and displays some attention deficit characteristics—distractibility, poor organization, impulsivity, and social immaturity—it is possible that ADD could account for his or her difficulties, even if he or she did well in early elementary school and is only now experiencing difficulty. It is important for parents and professionals who deal with older children to recognize that it is possible for teenagers to have problems that can be attributed to attention deficit. In fact, 20–25 percent of the children I evaluate are in this age group. These children undoubtedly had some attention deficit characteristics early on, but not severely enough to noticeably impair their academic performance in early elementary school.

These older children are extremely difficult to diagnose. When assessing students in the eleven- to sixteen-year-old group, I find that many of the characteristics that I look for in diagnosing younger children are gone. Fidgetiness and hyperactivity are not nearly as common with teens as with the younger children with attention deficit. On the other hand, certain attention deficit characteristics are considered normal for individuals as they enter adolescence. Teenagers are known for their impulsivity, lack of consistency, and mood fluctuations. The only sure way of differentiating between normal adolescent behavior and the symptoms of attention deficit is to have the child carefully evaluated in the manner discussed in Chapter Three—with educational, psychological, and neurodevelopmental assessments. A thorough evaluation should reveal any attention difficulties, learning disabilities, psychological problems, or neurodevelopmental delays that exist. If there are no difficulties in these areas, it is probably safe to assume that the child is just a typical teenager.

As with younger students, there are many reasons for the academic and behavioral problems of teenagers. If these difficulties are serious, parents need to seek the help of professionals in getting to the root of the problem and turning the child around before it is too late. There is a logical reason why some students with this type of deficit manage to do fine during the early years of their education and then experience problems as they enter junior high or high school. I believe that a new set of demands placed upon the student by the educational system is generally responsible for the precipitous decline of previously undiagnosed students with attention deficit, as well as some diagnosed students who were thought to have a very mild form of the disorder and were being treated without medication.

In the early elementary years, learning is mostly rote or passive. Material presented requires a great deal of "decoding," a term borrowed from Dr. Mel Levine. The decoding process breaks down whole concepts (either words or ideas) into parts, so the concepts are easier to understand, rules are mastered, and the ideas are memorized. If students do not understand a concept when it is introduced, the teacher presents the material over and over again. A student is continually exposed to similar information, and the ideas eventually sink in.

By the fifth and sixth grades, a child is being asked to become increasingly creative and to use much more analysis and personal expression, both in oral and in written work. Facts and material become increasingly autonomized to rapid memory, and organization becomes essential. The student must organize written projects from several sources and deal with mathematical problems in a much more complex method. Thus, an entirely new set of skills is necessary for survival in school.

Many of the teenage students who are referred to my learning evaluation center did reasonably well during the first several years in school but suddenly began to have difficulty in the fifth and sixth grades and proceeded to have very significant problems once they entered junior high school.

These older students fall into two distinct groups. Those in the first group have previously undiagnosed learning disabilities in addition to their attention deficit, and those in the second group have no learning disabilities.

I believe that the students in the first group were not diagnosed with learning disabilities earlier in their academic careers because once more analysis and writing are required in school, children with attention deficit, as all students, are forced to adapt new skills in order to be successful. With this sudden increase in demand for written or fine motor output, as well as an increased emphasis on rapid retrieval memory and receptive language ability, students with specific disabilities in these areas are suddenly in trouble. All of these skills were called upon much less frequently in the early elementary years, and, for that reason, instructors may have been totally unaware of such problem areas. Some children are able to get by until late elementary school before a teacher or counselor recognizes that specific disabilities exist.

The Teenager with Attention Deficit and Accompanying Learning Disabilities

The children in this first adolescent group with late onset attention deficit have certain learning disabilities that were probably unimportant to their success in school during the early years. These learning problems with encoding or synthesizing material became increasingly debilitating when accompanied by an attention problem, once the students approached junior high and high school.

Children with only a mild form of attention deficit, but who are well motivated and supported at home and at school can sometimes overcome their concentration problems without need for any other type of therapy. However, if the attention deficit is suddenly accompanied by a specific learning disability, often not apparent until middle childhood, the two together can cause more serious problems. Attention deficit together with a learning disability is often enough to overcome any coping techniques that a child has employed to offset either problem. This can spell disaster, leading to a great deal of frustration for that particular student, no matter how hard he or she tries.

The result is a formerly successful student who is suddenly labeled as "lazy" or "not motivated," or, worse, who begins to display behavioral problems. Such labels can have a devastating effect on a child's self-esteem, and, for a child this age, can lead to a perpetual downward spiral unless the student's problem is diagnosed and treated.

MARK

Mark is a large, well-developed, fifteen-year-old male who was referred to my learning evaluation center after having to repeat the eighth grade. The boy's academic failure had resulted in some extreme behavior, including involvement with drugs and alcohol and hanging out with the wrong crowd at school. Mark's mother appeared very helpless to do anything to influence this, and thus sought an independent evaluation to see if there were any measures that could assist her son.

A medical history revealed a normal pregnancy and delivery with no neonatal difficulties. Mark's developmental milestones were all considered to be within normal limits. However, there were some minor delays in speech development, which apparently disappeared by the time Mark was in school.

The child's family history was significant in that Mark's mother and biological father were divorced when the mother was four months pregnant. Mark has never seen his father and has never had any contact with him. The boy currently lives with his mother, stepfather, and younger half brother and half sister.

Mark's mother is very concerned that her son resembles his biological father in many characteristics. The father has had trouble holding on to a job, has been in and out of marriages, and has even been in jail several times. The mother worries that Mark may be headed in the same direction. His stepfather is also worried about the negative influence that Mark may have on their younger children.

In looking at Mark's evaluation, we first see an academic assessment including an intelligence test that indicated average to above-average intellectual ability. His achievement tests also showed excellent ability in mathematics, with notable delays in reading and written expression.

The next portion of the assessment, the neurodevelopmental evaluation, looked for specific areas of learning disability. This section also illustrated several valuable points. Mark appeared to have significant developmental or learning problems in several areas. The first was his fine motor ability: although the coordination of his fingers appeared adequate, Mark did have an awkward pencil grasp requiring a lot of pressure to control his writing. He also seemed to keep his eyes very close to the page to monitor his work, which made writing exceedingly slow and frustrating for him.

Another major area of delay was in visual retrieval, which represents difficulty with revisualization of material and obviously needs to become increasingly automatic as one progresses in school. Accurate visual retrieval is essential for rapid reading and spelling due to the necessity of a rapid sight word vocabulary for accomplishing this increased load of reading. It is also important in the formation of letters, which is essential in writing and becomes exceedingly important in the later school years, especially during timed exams.

Again, all of these areas have seemingly less relevance in the early elementary years. In early elementary school, Mark had most of his material presented in distinct blocks and with a lot of repetition, so that time was not of the essence in achieving early reading and writing skills. Also, much of the early reading was accomplished through a more phonetic basis, involving more blending together of syllables rather than a rapid retrieval from sight word vocabulary. The latter is obviously more dependent upon visual retrieval and a difficulty here would not show up until the later years.

The third area that showed up on the neurodevelopmental evaluation was selective attention. The checklist displayed performance approximately one standard deviation below normal for Mark's age. What is interesting is that Mark didn't begin to have significant problems until the later years of elementary school. Although his symptoms, including impulsivity, distractibility, and lack of attention to detail, were evident, the difficulty only became apparent as Mark began having learning difficulties in other areas. With the help of his family and with good ability, he was able to overcome most of these problems on his own until the later elementary years. It was only when he became overwhelmed by the other disabilities that his compensatory mechanisms no longer successfully enabled him to overcome his difficulties and his ability to perform nosedived.

As we can see, the problems in this group are unique and really represent a disorder that has often been referred to as "high output failure." By this, I mean an academic decline precipitated by increased demands—more classes, more classwork, and more homework. When attention deficit plays a role in this decline, the deterioration is of course more severe and more difficult to overcome than simply remediation of the specific learning disorders. Thus, again, we can see the necessity of an evaluation that takes into account all of these areas and tries to determine how significant each one is to the overall problem and what remedies are necessary.

The Teen Who Has Attention Deficit with No Learning Disabilities

The second type of adolescent who is diagnosed with attention deficit is a variation of the elementary school ADD child, with a perhaps milder form of attention deficit. This is usually an individual who is above average in intelligence and is from a very involved, motivated family. Most of the students in this latter group have no recognizable patterns of neurodevelopmental delay or learning disabilities that could account for their difficulties. Indeed, because of their backgrounds, several have numerous test reports that support the fact that these children are often of high-average to superior intelligence with no recognizable delays. However, what is interesting is that students in this second group frequently have academic and behavior histories similar to those of children in the group discussed above. The causes of the attention difficulties are somewhat different in the two groups, however, and certainly must be carefully identified in each child.

Children of this second type, during their earlier years in school, would have had more classical symptoms of a child with attention deficit, usually without the hyperactivity component. These children would have been inattentive in group settings, easily distracted in noisy environments, and have had a difficult time focusing in class. Why, then, do these students do well early on and begin to have significant difficulty in late elementary and junior high school, as opposed to the many children with attention deficit without hyperactivity who are diagnosed in the early elementary grades?

There seem to be two explanations for this in a child with no other learning disabilities. The first is that, as noted, these children often come from very motivated, high-achieving families who have sought out academic help all along the way to support them and provide them with a controlled environment. Many of these children are placed in private schools with smaller teacher/pupil ratios and notably fewer disruptions within the classroom routine. The ones not in private schools are often receiving individual tutoring after school or resource room assistance to make up for any material not picked up within the regular classroom. With all this support, these students fare pretty well in the early grades. Unfortunately, however, despite the help they receive, many of these students are unable to cope successfully with the increased demands of junior high or high school.

The second common characteristic we see in this group is that they tend to be quite bright and have been able to retain much of the material presented in early elementary school by listening maybe twenty or thirty percent of the time. Again, I have to emphasize that children with attention deficit at all levels display the normal variance in intellectual ability, ranging from moderately retarded to superior intelligence. What seems to be somewhat unique about this latter group is that many of these students cluster in the high-average to superior range, where it takes perhaps a bit longer for their coping techniques to be overwhelmed. With tutoring and smaller class size, these individuals are able to get by during the early years, paying attention perhaps one third of the time. Once they enter junior high school, the demands are greater, and their performance deteriorates, despite continual environmental manipulations and outside support.

TOM

An example of a child in this second group is Tom, an eleven-year-old, currently struggling in fifth grade. The earlier elementary years were somewhat difficult for Tom, but he always seemed to get through and was reasonably successful academically. Last year Tom had a great deal of difficulty in the fourth grade, barely managing to pass certain subjects, despite interventions. This year the difficulty has reached the point that Tom received three failing notices on his first six weeks report card. Because of this, the parents decided to obtain an evaluation to determine the reason for Tom's difficulties.

Tom was the product of a thirty-six-week pregnancy, resulting in fraternal twin delivery. Both boys weighed over six pounds and had no difficulty in the neonatal or infancy periods.

The parents stated that, toward the end of the first year of life, there were noted differences between the developing temperaments of the two boys. Tom always liked to have someone interacting with him. His brother, Rick, was much quieter and could entertain himself for prolonged periods of time.

As the boys progressed through the toddler years, their differences became even more evident. Tom was always on the go and preferred to explore, while Rick was content to watch cartoons or color. These patterns continued in preschool, although it was clear that both boys were exceedingly bright and caught on quite quickly to new ideas. In athletics, Tom was more aggressive and seemed to be the more gifted athlete, while Rick did not appear to get as much enjoyment from organized athletic pursuits.

In the early years in school, Tom began experiencing some difficulties. He appeared much less organized and less interested in academic accomplishments than his brother was. Tom would much rather be playing soccer or football, at which he clearly excelled.

When the boys reached third grade, their behavioral discrepancy became even more evident, as Tom took on the role of class clown and Rick was placed in honors classes for reading and math. Although Tom's academic advancement was certainly adequate, it came nowhere close to Rick's achievement. For this reason, Tom was placed in after-school tutoring, with some limitation of his athletic pursuits. This appeared to help temporarily, with immediate improvement in the quality of his work, which, unfortunately, was not sustained throughout the year.

The following summer, Tom received an academic evaluation which displayed a total IQ of 125 on the Wechsler test, with a verbal IQ of 128 and a performance IQ of 120. In this assessment, the subtests that required the most attention to detail were the most problematic for Tom.

As noted earlier, fourth grade was even more frustrating for him, and in fifth grade Tom began to fail in several areas. Despite tutoring and elimination of all extracurricular sports activities, his difficulties seemed to increase.

In our evaluation of Tom, several very significant findings emerged. First, in the academic assessment, we found that Tom's IQ scores were consistent, but his academic achievement scores displayed only grade level achievements in all areas despite his superior IQ. On the neurodevelopmental evaluation, Tom performed at or above his expected chronological age level on all areas of neurodevelopmental functioning, with excellent performance in visual motor integration, as well as short-term memory. However, on the selective attention checklist, Tom ranked greater than two standard deviations below the norm for his age. This checklist, as seen earlier, looks for classic characteristics we find in a child with an attention problem, such as distractibility, inability to complete work, impulsiveness, and poor organization.

The neurodevelopmental evaluation showed clearly that Tom displayed no areas of neurodevelopmental delay to account for the discrepancy between his IQ ability and achievement level. However, Tom's selective attention difficulties did indicate a late onset form of attention deficit disorder that was present early on but was compensated for by the boy's superior intelligence, as well as the extra assistance that he received both from his parents and from tutoring.

In completing the evaluations, Tom's psychological testing revealed a very spontaneous, likeable young man who had been exceedingly frustrated by his own inability to achieve in school. Tom was quite articulate and clearly able to express these feelings. When asked what he would wish for if given three wishes, Tom's first wish was that he might do well in school and please his parents. When Tom was asked to relate the most frustrating thing that people say to him, he immediately replied that he can't stand all adults telling him how smart he is, since, no matter how hard he tries, he is unable to successfully achieve in school.

What we see is a child with classical ADD and above-average intelligence, who obviously had characteristics consistent with a mild form of attention deficit in the early years, but was able to compensate for it by a lot of direction from his family, special assistance, and classroom and environmental manipulations. Once Tom reached an educational level that required more organization and self-control from the individual student, his compensatory mechanisms began to fail and his performance deteriorated accordingly. It should be noted that Tom displayed no learning disabilities on the neurodevelopmental exam and no particularly weak areas on the academic or achievement tests administered to him.

Summary

We are thus faced with two distinct groups of students that achieve a fair measure of success through the early elementary years, only to be increasingly overwhelmed and frustrated as they approach adolescence. Since these children often come from homes where achievement is highly valued, they receive the added pressure of parental frustration at a time when they are already struggling with the dependency/independency dichotomy, which is a universal dilemma for all of us as we proceed through adolescence. It is thus essential that we recognize this very distinct variation of attention deficit and get these students the help they need so that they can go on and be successful through junior high and later educational years. Losing these young people at this point makes it exceedingly difficult to ever reach them from an educational perspective.

The diagnosis of attention deficit in older students can come as a tremendous relief and can help to explain why school has been so difficult. Hopefully, with the proper support from parents and professionals, these students will be able to enjoy improved concentration and learning skills. Many will be able to go on to college, and I would like to close this chapter with some information about higher education.

Looking Ahead to College

As I have said repeatedly, there is no cure for attention deficit disorder, simply ways of coping with the problem. I cannot promise that every student with attention deficit who is fortunate enough to be diagnosed will succeed academically and will end up with a college degree. I can tell you, however, that there is hope.

There are many colleges that offer special programs for students with attention problems and learning disabilities. The list of schools is too lengthy to be printed in this book, and new programs are developed every year. For an up-to-date list of colleges that have programs for the learning disabled, contact the Association for Children and Adults with Learning Disabilities, 4156 Library Road, Pittsburgh, Pennsylvania 15234, (412) 341-1515. *A National Directory of Four-Year Colleges, Two-Year Colleges, and Post-High School Training Programs for Young People with Learning Disabilities*, edited by P. M. Fielding, is available from Partners in Publishing, Box 50347, Tulsa, Oklahoma 74150, (918) 584-5906. There is also *A Guide to Colleges for Learning Disabled Students*, edited by Mary Ann Liscio (Orlando, Florida: Academic Press, 1985). Help your child find out what a college can offer in the way of special classes, waivers of requirements, tutoring, and alternative examination formats.

You should also be aware of some special provisions for students with special learning needs who take the Scholastic Aptitude Test (SAT). This exam, which is required for admission to many colleges and universities, may be taken untimed, with a preceptor, and with other special considerations. For additional information regarding the SAT, write to the College Board, American Testing Program, Box 592, Princeton, New Jersey 08541.

Above all, help your teenager to prepare for higher education by sharpening her study skills. Encourage her to work at organization, notetaking, outlining, research, composition, and vocabulary. If your child has these skills, accompanied by self-confidence and determination, she will be starting college on the right foot.

7.

Medical Treatment: The Physician's Role in Treating Attention Difficulties

In the past twenty years, attention deficit has inspired more fad therapies and unsubstantiated treatment claims than probably any other pediatric/adolescent medical condition. The wide variety of fad treatments can be directly related to the chronic nature of the disorder and the fact that no single therapy, either medical or behavioral, comes close to providing a total cure. Many proponents of ADD remedies have meant well and have truly attempted to provide reasonable treatment options, but unfortunately, as I mentioned earlier, most of their therapies have been too narrow in focus, attempting to treat only certain aspects of attention deficit without looking at the disorder as a whole.

Other advocates of fad treatments have been less altruistic. They have perpetrated an alarming amount of misinformation for economic gain and/or personal fame, using seductive "miracle cure" claims to appeal to the vulnerability of anxious parents. As we have seen, attention deficit can evoke a tremendous amount of anxiety and distress in a family and can place parents in a compromised position. Because of their frustration and their zeal to find a quick and simple remedy, parents become easy prey to many of the outrageous claims that are put forth by some well-meaning and other less scrupulous individuals.

A Scientific Look
at Fad Treatments

Before examining the various medical and behavioral treatments available to us at this time, let us take a look at some of the fad therapies with a scientific eye. Separating out which treatment options are viable, which need careful medical scrutiny, and which are complete nonsense is often difficult, even for the most sophisticated medical observer.

Proposed therapies—whether for attention deficit or for other medical conditions—should be evaluated scientifically according to the following guidelines: (1) placebo vs. actual therapy trials (where one group of children receives the actual treatment and another group receives a treatment that appears to be similar but omits the specific intervention being studied), (2) random assignment of subjects, (3) double-blind methods (in which no group knows who is actually being treated and who is not), (4) standard evaluation (where each child is followed for a specific length of time so effects and side effects of treatment can be monitored), and (5) appropriate statistical analysis (where each study is looked at with careful accounting methods to determine the success rate).

It is up to the medical community to study each of these therapies, including the variety of medications that are being proposed to alleviate attention deficit. Only then should physicians decide which treatments are appropriate and which are unsubstantiated and therefore should not yet be recommended for patients.

THE FEINGOLD DIET

The first and best-known attempt at treating attention deficit in a more "natural" approach was the Feingold diet. Dr. Ben F. Feingold clearly stated that attention deficit has a genetic basis, which is certainly the case in most of my experiences. However, he went on to postulate that this genetic predisposition can somehow be modified by strict adherence to a diet free of food colors and additives, as well as of various salicylate-containing foods. A salicylate is a chemical related to aspirin that occurs naturally in such fruits and vegetables as peaches, apricots, plums, oranges, grapes, tomatoes, and cucumbers. Dr. Feingold felt that children with attention deficit had a level of sensitivity to salicylates, artificial flavorings, and synthetic food colorings that was so great that the slightest interruption of this diet could lead to immediate appearance of behaviors consistent with attention deficit.

These ideas were readily embraced with such conviction that, at one time, it was estimated that over a quarter of a million children were on the Feingold diet.

Following the publishing of Dr. Feingold's book, the scientific community set up multiple double-blind studies to attempt to substantiate his findings. Groups of children with attention deficit were divided up, and some of the children were restricted to the Feingold diet and were then compared with others who were not on this regimen. Once their food intake was carefully controlled, various capsules of dyes or salicylates were fed to these children, looking for changes in behavior. Unfortunately, after many similar studies in different universities and clinics, there were little scientific data to support Dr. Feingold's claims.

There is no question that a few children with attention deficit benefit from the Feingold diet. This could possibly be explained by the change in the way family members interrelate: the parents tend to place all blame on an external force, rather than constantly ridiculing the child for his behavior. In fact, parents may get so caught up in agonizing over diet that they don't even have time to notice the formerly annoying behaviors. Following this diet is clearly an all-encompassing family commitment, and it does seem to provide for more positive attention for the child with attention deficit.

But, again, well-designed studies with double-blind challenge tests fail to substantiate any ongoing effect from this regimen. Certainly, lowering food additives and artificial ingredients in a child's diet can be a healthful endeavor; however, following the extreme restrictions outlined in Dr. Feingold's book in the belief that it will cure a child's attention problems is misleading for most, and is disappointing to the vast majority of people who attempt it.

THE "NO SUGAR" APPROACH

Sugar restriction is probably the next most talked-about "miracle cure" in dealing with children who have attention deficit. Some people have considered an adverse reaction to sugar to be more directly linked to hyperactive children, feeling that sugar perpetuates these children's inattentiveness and aggressive behaviors. Indeed, many parents will testify that a child's behavior will deteriorate within a half hour of ingesting a large sugar load and that the child will be unbearable for the next several hours. In fact, in a few selected cases, this clearly seems to be true.

In the unusual circumstance that a particular child does respond adversely to sugar, then a diet that restricts sugar intake should definitely be followed. Certainly, limiting any child's sugar consumption will have multiple benefits to the teeth, to weight control, and in providing more adequate metabolic balance. However, restricting sugar with the belief that a child's attention deficit will be cured only sets up the family for additional frustration and disappointment in most cases.

A sugar avoidance diet can also place stress on a child by singling her out and making her "different" from the other kids. She can't eat her cupcake or cookies at the school party and has to pass up the cake and ice cream at her friend's birthday celebration. A child who has attention deficit is often different in other areas and does not need the added distinction of a special diet if it isn't going to improve her concentration.

In the multiple, double-blind placebo control studies that have looked at this problem, there is no clear proof of any association between sugar ingestion and subsequent behavioral alterations in children with attention deficit. According to a study recently published in *The American Journal of Psychiatry*, sugar consumption has no significant effect at all on children's behavior. The study looked at eighteen boys who reportedly reacted to sugar and twelve others who were thought to have no adverse effects from the substance. The children were observed both in a laboratory and at home, and their activity was measured by a device worn on a belt. Observers' ratings of the children's behavior indicated no direct relationship between sugar intake and hyperactivity.

OTHER NUTRITIONAL ANGLES

Along with the two misconceived theories of treating attention deficit described above, there are a variety of other nutritional approaches that have also been brought forth but have not been as readily embraced as the two we have looked at. Included among these is megavitamin ingestion. In one controlled study, children given large doses of vitamins actually showed an increase in disruptive classroom behavior. In addition to the misbehavior, these children displayed alarming metabolic side effects which included the increase of various hepatic (liver) enzymes with possible liver damage. Megavitamin therapy can definitely represent a danger and should be strongly discouraged for any child. There have also been advocates of a megamineral therapy that has potentially even greater toxic side effects and should be carefully avoided at this time.

A number of allergists and nutritionists have written about food allergies and even "brain allergies" as sources of attention problems. I do believe that much of the stress we place on our bodies due to sloppy eating habits has a detrimental effect in several areas, including behavior. Children who crave sugar have rapid glucose fluctuations in their blood, overworking the pancreas as well as the other systems that regulate glucose amounts in the bloodstream. However, to directly relate this to the cause of attention problems in most children does not have scientific validity at this time. Most children with attention deficit indeed do not crave sugar. Those who do, as we have seen, have very few adverse behavioral effects from the sugar. A small minority of children are adversely affected by sugar, and these few should avoid it. The same goes for wheat, salicylates, milk, and other allergens that have been implicated.

Children who experience undesirable behavioral reactions to foods represent only a small percentage of the children we are dealing with. All in all, I have not seen scientific data thus far to support the claims of the allergists and nutritionists who have tried to treat attention problems.

NEUROPHYSIOLOGICAL RETRAINING

Other theories that have been put forth include that of neuro-physiological retraining, which basically means that various patterning activities completed by children who have attention deficit will somehow "train" the brain and thus improve brain functioning. This idea is seen in such theories as that of Robert Doman and Carl Delacato, who believed that, if the child went through a pattern of exercises, he could retrain the brain by somehow providing missed sensory stimuli from early childhood and thus reprogram the brain's response. This is an interesting approach, but, again, we have no evidence of its effectiveness.

Dr. Jean Ayers has a theory with some similar concepts. She feels that much of the brain's processing is dependent upon the brain stem's ability to organize sensory input. With this idea in mind, she has designed techniques that initiate vestibular (the balance center) or tactile stimulation of areas of the brain to program them to work more efficiently. Dr. Ayers does have some well-established research, but she looks at only one area that may be contributing to the problem; she does not take into account all the complexities of attention deficit. Thus, although this therapy may help with the child's motor skills and coordination, it does little to deal with the underlying problems of inability to pay attention, complete tasks, and organize activities.

VISUAL TRACKING

A very controversial concept brought optometrists on the fad treatment parade. This theory was that visual tracking or optometric training could improve visual-perceptual skills, learning, and behavior. Optometrists have used programmed eye exercises as well as tedious pencil and paper tasks, such as mazes, that were to be done repeatedly in an attempt to decrease the amount of time required for the task. These activities were developed in an effort to treat various learning disabilities, but they have also been mentioned in relation to attention deficit.

Even more recently, optometrists have used tinted lenses in glasses in order to assist children in overcoming reading and attention problems. "Seeing the world through rose-colored glasses" may sound appealing, but it only serves to make things look pink. There are no scientific data to indicate that the procedure enables a child to read or concentrate any better.

Optometrists have also developed a couple of fad therapies involving focus during movement. In one type of treatment, children are told to jump up and down on a trampoline for fifteen to twenty minutes and to focus their eyes on a stable object. In a similar therapy, a child is placed on a rotating bed and is told to concentrate on a stable object or picture on the ceiling.

No scientific studies have proven that these focusing or eye exercise therapies have any beneficial effect on children's reading or attention skills. The activities are not harmful and, in fact, may be helpful, redirecting a child who "bounces off the wall" to bouncing on a trampoline instead. The problem is that the sole focus of such an activity is visual tracking; these optometric exercises ignore all other aspects of the child's difficulties. Of course, such a narrowly focused approach has been shown to be ineffective in treating a child with attention difficulties.

In 1984, after careful research, three independent branches of medicine released a joint statement commenting on the evidence against the effectiveness of visual training for treating attention deficit. The American Academy of Pediatrics, the American Academy of Ophthalmology (the branch of medicine dealing with functions, structure, and diseases of the eye) and Otolaryngology (the branch of medicine dealing with diseases of the ear, nose, and throat), and the American Association of Ophthalmology all stated that this treatment has minimal value. Yet hundreds of optometrists are charging outrageous sums for this therapy.

CHIROPRACTIC TREATMENT
Unfortunately, there is more. Chiropractors have also entered the arena of the "learning disability specialist." They claim that by

using a certain type of manipulation ("applied kinesiology") they can reverse many learning disabilities, including attention problems.

There is absolutely no scientific research to substantiate their claim. The form of head, neck, and spinal manipulation they advise is based on theoretical assumptions that are completely hypothetical and actually go against many known anatomical facts. However, despite what seem to be erroneous conclusions based on unproven suppositions, some chiropractors continue to make money because of people's fears and needs for help.

Many proponents of therapies previously discussed certainly sought to come up with viable treatment alternatives in an effort to help children with attention deficit. Unfortunately, however, none of their theories has been scientifically shown to provide any consistent assistance for the majority of these children. Parents should look to concerned health professionals and educators for help in understanding these theories and for protection against many of the unsubstantiated claims that often surround them.

Therapies That Work

Let's look at the various types of therapy that *are* effective in treating this complex disorder. I will begin with a discussion of medical therapy; subsequent chapters will examine behavioral and educational therapies.

Again, I must emphasize the importance of a team approach, for only when we combine medical, behavioral, and educational treatments into one coordinated effort will we achieve the most favorable outcome possible. Once a child is diagnosed, an appropriate therapy will require the same amount of team cooperation. By combining medical treatment with behavioral modification and appropriate educational adjustments, our success rate can indeed be, and has been, consistently high and gratifying for all.

What to Tell
Your Child about ADD

When treatment is initiated, it is important for the child to have an understanding of his attention deficit problems, if at all possible. The child needs to know that his academic problems are not his fault. He is not having trouble in school because he is lazy or doesn't try hard enough, and he is not "bad" or "dumb." Let him know that you know that he is doing the very best he can, but he has a problem that makes it hard for him to concentrate and get his work done. Explain to your child that every person is unique, and that we *all* have certain strengths and weaknesses.

It will help your child to know that concentration is not his strong point, and that paying attention does not come easily for him. He will have to work at it. But the fact that he has a concentration problem does not mean that he is not intelligent or a good child. Although he may envy his friends who breeze through their schoolwork and make straight A's, he may find that they wish they had his talent for sports, art, music, or another field.

Let your child know *why* it is difficult for him to pay attention. Tell him as much about attention deficit as he is capable of understanding, and as he gets older, tell him more. For example, you can explain attention deficit to your six-year-old this way: "Billy, I want you to understand why it's hard for you to listen to your teacher and get your work done at school. Everyone's body has tiny parts that work like mailmen and deliver messages to the brain. Your body doesn't use enough of those mailmen, and some of your messages get mixed up. Even though your ears can hear what your teacher is saying, her words may not really get through to your brain because some other message may get there instead. This isn't your fault. It's just the way your body is."

It is also important for your child to know that he is not the only one in the world with this problem and that there are a lot of kids in his school who have attention deficit problems. If you know that other people in his family have ADD, it might help to share that information too. Assure your child that there are many children, parents, and even teachers who have attention problems; he is not alone. Be sure to convey that it's O.K. for him to be the way he is, and that you love him just the way he is—and always will.

Let your child know that you, his teacher, and his doctor are going to help him. Even a very young child, when counseled by parents and/or a physician, can be helped to recognize his own undesirable behaviors and academic problems. He can be given certain cues when he is distracted or when his conduct is starting to get out of hand, so that he will know when he needs to work at concentrating or behaving more appropriately.

Depending on your child's age and the severity of his inattention, the doctor may want to prescribe medication that will improve your child's concentration. Medical help can be a welcome relief. If you choose this route, I would urge you to be honest with your child about the purpose for the medication. Don't say that it is candy, a vitamin, or an allergy pill. You should explain to your child that the medication will make it easier for him to concentrate, complete his assignments, and get along with his friends.

It is important to tell your child, however, that the medication will not solve all of his problems; it cannot do everything for him. I often tell my patients, "This pill will not make you smarter. It doesn't need to. You are already smart enough. It will help you, though. The medicine will make it easier for you to pay attention to your teacher and your schoolwork. If you work very hard, you will probably finish your assignments and do better in school." That last sentence is the key one: this will take hard work.

Be sure your child realizes that he is responsible for his own actions. As his schoolwork improves, give him the praise that he deserves. When he lags behind or misplaces his assignments, offer incentives for getting the work turned in. Don't let your child use forgotten or worn-off medication as an excuse for inappropriate actions or for failure to attempt academic achievement.

Likewise, I would urge you, as a parent or an educator, to refrain from making comments that link a child's undesirable behaviors to a need for medication. It is best not to say, "You're acting like you need some more medicine," or "You wouldn't have done that if you'd taken your medicine today." The medicine should never be regarded as a puppeteer pulling the child's strings. Although we can all appreciate the tremendous benefits of the medication, the child must know that he is still in control of his actions and is truly responsible for his academic and social accomplishments; he is also ultimately responsible for his short-comings.

Another common problem we face today is a by-product of our drug-oriented society. Children are taught from an early age to "say 'no' to drugs." Parents need to make a clear distinction between street drugs and medications prescribed by doctors.

Medical Treatment of Attention Deficit

Keeping that in mind, let us take a look at the medical treatments available for attention deficit. We have come a long way in the past ten years in understanding many of the aspects of attention deficit with the knowledge that we can make a significant difference. With the proper diagnostic approaches and careful monitoring of the patients, we can have a very significant impact on the quality of life and future potential for these individuals.

First, in looking at the medical aspects of treatment, I will begin with a small qualifier. As I have stressed throughout the book, attention deficit is a continuum that, as in any medical problem, has a tremendous range. This entity can vary extensively, as we have seen, from the case of the mildly inattentive child to that of the severely impulsive, distractible individual. The more mildly affected individuals can sometimes be controlled with appropriate environmental manipulation, and whether these individuals should also seek appropriate medical treatment should be a decision carefully made by the parents, physician, and, when appropriate, the child. However, I do believe that the majority of the children who are properly diagnosed as having attention deficit will be assisted by medication.

For years, many adults have inadvertently treated mild forms of attention deficit with caffeine. I have had several parents mention that their children do better at school after drinking two cups of coffee at breakfast. The beneficial effect of caffeine is understandable, since caffeine is a stimulant and can aid to some degree in the stimulation of neurotransmitters. A grandmother recently reported to me that, whenever the family gathers at her home for a holiday or celebration, she immediately makes a strong cup of coffee for her eight-year-old grandson. This apparently assures a more peaceful day. Another grandmother told me that she has started giving her grandson a cup of coffee before each soccer game and has noticed a remarkable improvement in his play. Some children who need medication may benefit from its combined use with caffeine, but the same positive response could probably be obtained by slightly increasing the dosage of the medication. Unfortunately, the effect of caffeine on children is usually quite mild. For most children, caffeine doesn't make a noticeable difference at all. We therefore do not recommend this as part of our treatment.

The correct and appropriate treatment, on the other hand, can have a potentially tremendous benefit for anyone who has attention deficit. With that in mind, let us begin to explore some of the medical treatment alternatives at the various ages and how each particular age group offers challenge in treatment as well as in diagnosis. We must remember, and I will continue to stress, that although these drugs can be enormously helpful in assisting children who have attention deficit, they are never a miracle cure by themselves. They must be incorporated into a system of behavioral and educational support. Then, and only then, can they assert their maximal benefit.

STIMULANT MEDICATIONS

We discussed in Chapter Two some of the theories as to how stimulant and similar therapies seem to work from a physiological perspective. Methylphenidate (generic name), or Ritalin (brand name), appears to stimulate the release of the reserve pool of neurotransmitters to increase the ability to pay attention and focus. Certain research has suggested that dextroamphetamine

(Dexedrine), on the other hand, a psychostimulant medication similar to methylphenidate, appears to decrease the uptake of these neurotransmitters and thus increase their effect at the nerve endings. In other words, dextroamphetamine works in a different way to achieve the same effect of increasing the amount of neurotransmitters. Pemoline, or Cylert, also has a similar effect, but we do not yet know exactly how or where it acts. There are several medications currently being used for attention deficit and others that are beginning to be used. I will begin with a brief discussion of each of these and then go on to some clinical applications.

Methylphenidate (Ritalin)

Methylphenidate, or Ritalin, is by far the most frequently used medication and the most extensively studied. As we have seen, methylphenidate seems to stimulate the release of neurotransmitters and thus improve concentration. Neither children nor adults develop an addiction to methylphenidate, nor does there appear to be a tolerance developed once the desired dosage is attained. One of the advantages of methylphenidate is that the response is immediate. Once the appropriate dosage is attained, not only do we see increased selective attention, but, with the proper support, these individuals often become calmer, with decreased mood alterations, fewer uncontrolled tantrums, and less impulsivity, as well as better organization.

Appropriate doses to produce these desired effects vary between .3 milligrams per kilogram (2.2 pounds) of body weight and one milligram per kilogram of body weight per 24-hour period. This is usually provided in two to three divided doses throughout the day, depending on the age (and maturity) of the individual. I have found that, for the majority of individuals, a dose between .5 and .8 milligrams per kilogram seems to be the most beneficial with minimal side effects. In other words, if your child weighs 44 pounds, her weight in kilograms is 20. I would recommend starting her on a dose between five and ten milligrams, knowing that ten or 20 milligrams per day will probably be the effective dose. Occasionally larger doses are needed for particular individuals; however, these are not the norm.

Methylphenidate is available in a sustained release form that is marketed as a medication to help a child during school hours. The duration is supposed to be six hours. Older children may need a small afternoon dose to help them concentrate on homework. Sustained Release Ritalin is three times as expensive as the regular Ritalin, and, in my experience, it has never been shown to have a significantly longer duration or any therapeutic advantage.

Side effects with methylphenidate include appetite suppression, which is usually more pronounced initially but fades as the child becomes accustomed to the medicine. Occasionally, this can lead to some weight loss that can usually be controlled by ensuring that the child eats a good breakfast and dinner with encouragement of nutritious after-school and bedtime snacks. Since the half-life (duration of action) of methylphenidate is short, and its maximal effect is only three to four hours, dosing around mealtimes can usually be adjusted to avoid weight loss from decreased appetite.

The other side effect of methylphenidate on children with attention deficit is a decrease in growth velocity. It appears that in some individuals there may be a decrease in growth velocity for the first year or two, but afterwards the growth rate returns to normal. I have found, and this has been substantiated in the literature, that "drug holidays," especially for all or part of the summer, provide a catch-up period for these children. Ultimately, these patients will reach the projected adult height.

I have not found decreased growth to be a major problem of children I have treated, and, with the proper adjustment for catch-up periods, the medication's benefits certainly seem to outweigh any possible disadvantages. However, this is one aspect of the therapy that should be closely monitored by the physician with frequent measurements of both height and weight.

Another initial side effect that we occasionally see is the child becoming very moody and irritable for the first hour or two after the medication has worn off, which is usually after school. In most cases, we see this only for the first two or three weeks that the child is on the medication. In some cases, this problem is severe and necessitates adjusting the medication or adding a small dose after school. In a very small minority of cases, it will be necessary to discontinue the medication or change to another type.

Dextroamphetamine (Dexedrine)

There are two other stimulant medications that are being used to treat attention deficit: dextroamphetamine (Dexedrine) and pemoline (Cylert). Dextroamphetamine, in particular, is being prescribed for increasing numbers of patients.

Dextroamphetamine, especially in the spansule (capsule) form, has a notably long duration of action, which is useful with some older children who do not want to take a second dose at school. Adolescents in particular seem to tolerate this medication well. This prolonged effect seems to be more reproducible than that of the methylphenidate slow-release tablets, which I have not found to be particularly more helpful than the regular methylphenidate.

The side effects of dextroamphetamine, however, are more significant in school-age children and keep this medication from being the drug of first choice for many patients who are in their early years of elementary school. Side effects include some sedation and mood alterations, and, like methylphenidate, this medication can also cause some appetite suppression.

These side effects, however, are much less common in older children. In fact, dextroamphetamine is my drug of choice for the treatment of teenagers. Younger children who have attention deficit with hyperactivity and with a conduct disorder will do better on dextroamphetamine.

The dosage for the spansules is usually half that of methylphenidate, or .15 to .5 milligrams per kilogram of body weight. The most common dosage is approximately .3 or .35 milligrams per kilogram. If your child weighs 110 pounds (50 kilograms), she will need between 7.5 and 25 milligrams of dextroamphetamine per day. The optimal dosage for a child of that size will probably be 15–20 milligrams daily. Dexedrine comes in three sizes (five, ten, and 15 milligram spansules), which makes it far more convenient than the Ritalin SR (sustained release), which comes in only one size (20 milligrams).

Pemoline (Cylert)

Pemoline, the last of the stimulants, also has the advantage of a much longer duration than that of methylphenidate. The effect of pemoline is sustained for a greater time period and requires only a once-a-day dosage.

The disadvantage of this medication is that the amount of improvement for most individuals appears to be notably less than with methylphenidate or dextroamphetamine. Pemoline also takes one to two weeks to reach an appropriate level, and its effect, if present, may not even be recognizable until after a few weeks of treatment.

Dosage used from pemoline ranges between 18.75 milligrams (½ of a 37.5 milligram tablet, which is the most common form) to 112.5 milligrams per day, with 37.5 to 75 milligrams usually successful in early elementary and 75 to 112.5 milligrams daily in later elementary and junior high students.

As I mentioned earlier, many individuals with attention deficit and rapid mood fluctuations may have difficulty tolerating methylphenidate, since it may accentuate their moodiness. A trial of pemoline for this type of child may be warranted.

TRICYCLIC ANTIDEPRESSANTS

The next broad class of medications used is the tricyclic variety, a class of medications often prescribed for depressive illnesses in adults. These medications, although used infrequently for attention deficit, have begun to assume a slightly more significant role. The two most commonly used are imipramine (Tofranil) and desipramine (Norpramin). There is evidence that their mechanism of action appears to be the blocking of the breakdown of the neurotransmitters that pass messages from one brain cell to another. Thus, in a sense, the tricyclics have a similar effect as the stimulants.

Side effects seem to be fewer than with the stimulant medications; however, there is some dryness of the mouth and a slight increase in heart rate or blood pressure, which do not appear to be significant in low doses. In my experience, these medications have a more noticeable impact on hyperactive children with significant depressive components or conduct disorders than on children with other forms of attention deficit.

The difficulty is that there is a tolerance that appears to develop in this class of medication that doesn't exist in the stimulants. A certain dosage will be fine for awhile, but slowly it begins to lose its effect. To sustain a good response the dosage needs to be gradually increased. This makes it necessary to monitor the children closely as we increase the dosage throughout the year. I have found that, if we do this gradually, we can get through a nine-month school year and then, by discontinuing the medication for four to six weeks during the summer, the tolerance seems to disappear. If this does not occur, some physicians suggest switching from one class of tricyclics to another, which will also decrease the tolerance.

I usually start a child out at one milligram per kilogram of body weight, but have found that a dosage from two up to five milligrams per kilogram produces the most beneficial effect. Once one approaches three to four milligrams per kilogram of body weight, an electrocardiogram (EKG) should be performed and cardiac function monitored. Some physicians will get an EKG before starting tricyclics to be sure the heart rate is perfectly normal. With larger doses, cardiac conduction defects have been found; these, however, are rare.

TEGRETOL

New therapies are always being proposed to help children who have attention deficit; two medications that are most interesting and have been written about recently are Tegretol and Clonidine.

Tegretol is a common anticonvulsant used for many forms of seizure disorders. It has been discovered that children who have both attention deficit and a seizure disorder (which is very rare) can benefit from using Tegretol alone. This seems to decrease not only their seizures but their attention problems as well. It is thus being advocated by some neurologists as a primary treatment for attention deficit. I have personally not seen sufficient data to support this or to recommend its use at this time.

CLONIDINE

A medication that may offer a little more promise is Clonidine, which you may recognize since it is used to help control high blood pressure in adults. The drug has also been used with a syndrome known as Tourette's. Attention problems and hyperactivity are included among the symptoms of many individuals with Tourette's Syndrome, and Clonidine has been shown to control some of these inattentive hyperactive characteristics in Tourette's patients. Clonidine is currently being experimented with in children with attention deficit and hyperactivity, but without the other manifestations of Tourette's. The initial results have appeared to be positive in some cases, which indicates that, hopefully, this medication will provide a future alternative in helping children who have ADDH.

Clonidine also has a stimulant effect on certain neurotransmitters, which may be responsible for its actions. It rapidly breaks down and usually needs to be given several times during the day, similar to methylphenidate. Prolonged treatment has not been shown to lead to tolerance, which is most beneficial in establishing a dosage.

Another benefit of Clonidine is that it appears to have a positive effect on appetite. Parents do not need to be concerned that their children will lose weight or have growth problems on this medication, since Clonidine seems to stimulate appetite, rather than suppress it.

There are, however, several areas of possible concern regarding the use of Clonidine. Since this medication has been used by adults to decrease blood pressure, physicians need to monitor the blood pressure of children on this medication. However, I have not found this to be a problem in the small group of children whom I have successfully treated with Clonidine.

Another area of concern is that, in large doses, Clonidine can cause excessive fatigue. For this reason, I start patients out on a small dose at bedtime of ½ of a .1 milligram tablet. This does not affect the child during the day, but it allows him to get accustomed to the effect of the medication. After three or four days, the child begins to take ¹/₂ tablet in the morning as well as ¹/₂ tablet at bedtime. Finally, the child is able to take ¹/₂ tablet three or four times a day. Occasionally, larger doses are needed, but the medication must be increased very gradually due to the fatigue. Unfortunately, this fatigue factor often makes it impossible to achieve a dosage that will improve the child's concentration.

It is also important to note that Clonidine should never be prescribed for a child with attention deficit who is depressed. This medication has been known to worsen depression and should be avoided for such children.

I have prescribed Clonidine for several children who did not respond favorably to the psychostimulants. So far, there have been mixed reviews. Some patients have been helped, but others have received no benefits from this medication. Clonidine seems to provide a positive alternative for those who do not benefit from some of the other drugs. However, it is only an alternative. We do not yet have enough long-term information on the medication to use it as a first or even a second choice drug.

TREATING THE PRESCHOOLER

In looking at the medical aspect of treating individuals who have attention deficit, I once again have found it useful to divide these children by age groups to delineate the most beneficial effects of therapy. I will begin with the preschoolers, who pose a few problems.

I mentioned earlier that children in this age group are easy to diagnose and hard to treat. I will qualify the first part of that statement by acknowledging a problem with diagnosis. Although preschoolers with attention deficit are generally easy to spot because of their high activity level or their misconduct, there are many children who do not have ADD but are also very active and behave in a similar way. The difference is that those children who do not have attention deficit generally will be able to concentrate long enough to listen to a whole story, to sing several songs, or to finish a picture. There is a great deal of variability in development during the preschool years. Children without attention deficit who are extremely active in preschool may settle down significantly before they get to first grade, while those who have attention deficit will continue to have trouble in school.

Before getting into the treatment of preschoolers, I must tell you that I rarely recommend medication for children in this age group. Most of these kids can concentrate and behave well enough to get by in preschool, since there is not a great deal of academic emphasis at this level. For these children, I suggest that parents use behavior management techniques (which will be outlined in Chapter Eight) and that teachers implement some of the classroom management suggestions in Chapter Ten.

Unfortunately, there are a few preschool children who desperately need medical assistance. These children are the ones who are so hyperactive and/or temperamental that they pose a threat to themselves or to others. These are the children who jump out of windows, run in front of cars, get up and go outside in the middle of the night, and injure other children. Frequently, parents don't know what to do with these children, and their families are in turmoil. After trying everything else, medication becomes a necessary last resort.

In Chapter Three we looked at two distinct groups of hyperactive preschool children with attention deficit (ADDH)—those who have no accompanying conduct disorders and those with significant conduct disorders. As I have said, I recommend medication for children in these groups only when the children are a threat to themselves, their friends, or the stability of their families.

The first group of individuals frequently seen in the preschool category, and by far the most common, are the hyperactive children without conduct disorders. These children will usually respond very well to stimulants, although frequently much better to methylphenidate or dextroamphetamine than to pemoline.

Usually, on a twice-a-day dosage of short-acting methylphenidate or perhaps a Dexedrine spansule, these individuals, with the appropriate behavioral support, can do quite well both academically and socially. It should be noted that, occasionally, these individuals will have some mood swings in the afternoon when coming off these medications; however, this side effect tends to become less significant after two or three weeks, as we noted earlier.

Fortunately, I see fewer hyperactive preschoolers who have conduct disorders. Children with significant conduct disorders have a less than ideal response to stimulant medications; however, some of these children do well on dextroamphetamine. Generally, these children seem to do better on the tricyclic medications such as imipramine and desipramine. It must be remembered, however, that tolerance is built up to these medications, so one has to monitor these children closely, usually having to increase the dosage moderately throughout the year to sustain its positive effect. Because of this, Clonidine may provide a new and useful option for these children, but our experience with this medication is still limited.

Children with attention deficit accompanied by conduct disorders are perhaps the most difficult ADD children to manage. They are often very bright individuals who are a constant challenge to all who deal with them. A great deal of support and cooperation from physicians, instructors, parents, and often psychologists can help in developing the appropriate environment for these children at school as well as at home.

TREATING THE
EARLY ELEMENTARY SCHOOL CHILD

The children with attention deficit looked at in Chapter Five were those who first display concentration problems in early elementary school. These are the disorganized children who can't finish their school work and have trouble focusing in class. This group, if caught early, before many of the secondary manifestations of frustration and low self-esteem develop, can also have an excellent response to therapy. Again, I usually use methylphenidate as my drug of first choice. If these children are properly evaluated and treated on all levels, behaviorally and medically, they usually respond quite well.

Here we can use a two- to three-times-a-day dosage, depending upon the amount of homework or extracurricular activity. Many patients with attention deficit have found that medication will help them to concentrate and focus better in all activities, including athletics. They will thus take a dose before a football game on Friday night or a soccer game on Saturday. This should not be discouraged. If the medication has a positive effect for both school and social development, there is no reason not to benefit from it after school or on weekends when desired. This medication should be recognized as a support that, when used and monitored carefully, can have a positive effect on many aspects of the child's life.

The school-age child with ADDH may occasionally need additional support as the academic demands increase. Those children not diagnosed early enough may have some secondary characteristics of depression resulting from failure, and particularly if they have been controlled either on tricyclic or stimulant alone, they may begin to have problems again. I have found that combining a lower dose of each of these medications together can be very advantageous for these children's academic achievement and social interaction. By using smaller doses of both medications, one can eliminate many of the side effects from each and get a combined, or synergistic, response. This simply means that the two medications work together to produce a greater response than one would get from either medication by itself. It must be remembered that this method is useful for only a select few, but when appropriate I have found the approach quite successful.

Occasionally, I have used pemoline with children diagnosed in the elementary age group who do not tolerate methylphenidate due to severe mood swings. These individuals appear to have a more even and long-lasting response to pemoline than to methylphenidate. Since pemoline seems to have a more sustained duration of action, these children do not experience the mood fluctuations. In this select group, I have achieved a moderate success with pemoline, although the effects of this medication are milder and can take one or two weeks to appear, making it difficult to predict pemoline's effectiveness.

Dextroamphetamine seems to cause more side effects in young elementary school children. Sometimes, a child who does not respond to methylphenidate will have a positive response to dextroamphetamine spansules, but this is not my first choice of medication for this age group.

TREATING THE TEENAGER
The final group are those children who begin to experience attention difficulties in middle childhood, rather than those who have been diagnosed earlier and have reached middle childhood. Those diagnosed in preschool or early elementary will continue to be treated on the regimens that have been successful for them. But the children who are first diagnosed in their teen years represent a unique challenge for treatment.

With this middle childhood group, I have had much more success using dextroamphetamine first. This group does not appear to manifest the withdrawal mood alterations that younger children experience, and they seem to benefit from dextroamphetamine's longer duration of action in the spansule form.

Many of these children, who suffer from depression as well as attention difficulty, benefit from the tricyclics. However, I usually refer these patients to my psychiatric colleagues. Teens with attention deficit who are depressed certainly need some ongoing psychotherapy in addition to medication.

Occasionally, in treating an adolescent case, I have been successful with a slightly larger dose of pemoline, usually three to three and one half 37.5 milligram tablets daily; however, I have not found this to be nearly as universally effective as the dextroamphetamine.

There are several new medications now being experimented with that I have not discussed. These medications still need to be thoroughly evaluated before they are used in clinical practice.

The Controversy over Medication

Pharmacological therapy is perhaps the most controversial attention deficit treatment, and, unfortunately, for all the wrong reasons. The reality of the situation is that there are no miracle cures, nor could we expect one for a disorder that has such deep physiological, psychological, and sociological roots.

I think one of the reasons some of the medication that is used for attention deficit has gotten a bad name is that many drugs have been used after inappropriate assessments on children with inattentiveness who don't have ADD at all.

Some of the drugs, amphetamines in particular, have been abused by adults and have been placed on the controlled substance list. Serious drug abuse problems developed during the late 1960s when more and more young adults began using these medications as "diet pills" and discovered that high dosages, especially when taken intravenously, could result in feelings of euphoria.

The use of amphetamines and methylphenidate is now regulated by the U.S. government. Physicians may write prescriptions for only controlled amounts (specified by state law) with no refills, and telephone orders are illegal. I am mentioning this regulation of stimulant medications because it has been necessitated by adult abuse in the past.

Parents can be assured that these medications, when administered properly, are nonaddictive and are usually very helpful for children with attention deficit. When a health professional takes the trouble to adequately diagnose the problem, the likelihood of success in helping these individuals is much greater than the seventy-five percent number often referred to in the literature. Children whom I have carefully evaluated and diagnosed have had a positive response to medication more than nine out of ten times.

Parents of children with attention deficit who have been carefully evaluated and monitored can be confident that the stimulant medications are safe and are usually very effective, tending to calm children down and increase their attention spans. Some of the most outspoken critics of medical treatment for attention deficit have been the very people who have brought us such therapies as sugar avoidance, megavitamins, or eye exercises to cure this obviously complex and frustrating problem. I wish I could say that all of the other treatments that are advocated for the therapy of attention deficit were as helpful and as safe as stimulant medications are. The fact is that most of these fad therapies are too limited in approach to be beneficial, and a few could even be dangerous. As I have said before, it is essential that you find a knowledgeable, caring team of professionals who can provide your child with therapy that has been proven to be safe and effective.

Summary

In summary, one can see that the medical treatment of attention deficit is an exciting and fascinating science with knowledge and techniques appearing very rapidly. It is therefore imperative that parents and professionals form an alliance and combine all aspects of treatment to ensure a successful outcome. We have many tools and a great deal of knowledge available to us that was not present even five or ten years ago. We need to coordinate these resources to provide maximum benefits for all individuals involved; attention deficit affects not only school, but all areas of an individual's life.

8.

The Parent's Role in Treating Attention Difficulties

Many children who are diagnosed as having attention deficit will be started on medical treatment, which, hopefully, will have an immediate positive effect. Of course, that treatment cannot erase the anger, frustration, and lack of self-esteem that the child has experienced prior to therapy. Paying attention to this psychological aspect of attention deficit is an essential part of any treatment process, and if this is neglected the child's response to medication, although positive at first, will certainly diminish over time.

A good analogy is the treatment of a child with diabetes. Insulin will lower the child's blood sugar, but the medication will not control the problem if the child lives on a steady diet of cake and cola. Diabetic children, like children with attention deficit, need effective behavioral guidance if their treatment is to achieve long-lasting success.

Children who have attention deficit are often raised from an early age on a steady diet of what not to do. These children may think that "no" is the most widely used word in the English language, and from their perspective, it certainly is! The mother of one of my patients recently told me that her four-year-old daughter was so accustomed to hearing the word "no" following her name that she thought it was part of her name. When the child was asked what her name was by some friends of her parents, she replied, "Dana No."

This type of negativity is difficult to avoid, even under the best of circumstances. Throughout their childhood, children with attention deficit frequently test every limit, and they rarely accomplish any task on time. As we have seen, such behaviors can vary and are certainly more evident in hyperactive children than in children who have attention deficit without hyperactivity. However, this early frustration and difficulty in adapting to adult expectations is usually present to some degree in all of these children.

Allowing students with attention deficit to assume some responsibility for their actions and getting parents and instructors involved in a positive, objective manner can go a long way toward easing frustration. A positive approach can also help these children build a badly needed sense of self-esteem.

Can He Help It?

You are no doubt wondering to what degree your child with attention difficulties can be held accountable for his actions. Can he help the way he acts? Is it fair to punish him for things over which he may have little control?

This is a tough one—should you relate attention-seeking behaviors to a physical cause and thus not hold the child responsible, or is this actually more of a psychological disorder that stems from a biologically based attention problem? There is no easy way to separate all this out and understand your child's behavior. Some "authorities" advise against punishing a child for a behavior that is related to his temperament. These individuals contend that behaviors such as hitting, biting, kicking, whining, and throwing tantrums are temperamental behaviors and are thus out of the child's control. I agree with them to an extent, but some children purposely use these types of behavior to gain control and get what they want. An action that is truly temperamental on one occasion may be manipulative the next time around.

For instance, let's say that five-year-old Johnny loses his temper and clobbers his sister. Perhaps you, as the parent, decide that he couldn't help himself. After taking care of the injured sibling, you give Johnny a hug and tell him that you understand how angry he felt and why he felt like he had to hit his sister. Even though you go on to tell him that you want him to show his anger in a more acceptable manner next time, you have given Johnny some positive attention, and sometime in the future when he wants some attention he may remember this and hit his sister again.

So how are you going to know when your child's behavior cannot be helped? You probably won't know for sure; you'll just need to do your best to assess the situation and determine your own course of action. If your child's behavior is physically aggressive and harmful to others or to himself, I would recommend punishment by one of the methods that will be outlined later in this chapter. After all, the child does have to go to school and eventually become part of society.

There is no question that a child psychologist can begin to aid the family in dealing with many of the physically based problems that can be approached from a psychological basis. A psycho-educational approach that combines psychological and educational therapies with appropriate medical treatment (if needed) can be very successful with the child who has attention deficit. This type of therapy seems to produce the best overall results because it addresses the most significant aspect of the attention deficit phenomenon—getting the child to focus so he can learn effectively and interact with his peers successfully.

A Positive Parental Approach

Parents should adopt a positive approach in their interactions with their children. As noted earlier, because children with attention difficulties often act impulsively and behave inappropriately, they tend to receive a tremendous amount of negative attention from adult authority figures. The testing of limits often locks parents and child into a continual struggle, with hollering, huge family fights, and other negative behavior.

In most cases, a negative parental response is understandable, since children with attention deficit are frequently difficult to manage. Even the ones without hyperactivity and without conduct disorders have their trying moments. These children can be insatiable, argumentative, stubborn, and immature, as we have seen. Many of these children display what psychologists call oppositional behavior, going against whatever the parent wants. Children with attention deficit frequently have a very low threshhold for frustration and "erupt" when thwarted in whatever their ambitions may be at the time. Inevitably, parents will lose their patience and respond in a negative fashion.

It is a proven fact that negative reinforcement is not as effective as a positive approach. For that reason, it is essential that parents change from a negative approach to a positive style of discipline—which certainly is easier to talk about than to implement.

A primary goal of parenting should be to help the child achieve success. Success for the child who has attention deficit, as well as for any other child, should be measured by effort. Parents should encourage children to do *their* best, not to be *the* best. Parents should show pride in their children's successes, no matter how small, and should give their children opportunities to succeed in different areas. I would encourage you to offer praise and give rewards generously and frequently. If you praise your child for trying, even when she doesn't succeed, she is likely to continue to try.

That part may not seem so hard. It's living with the child day in and day out that wears a parent down. Children with attention deficit have all the normal behavior problems plus . . . ! Dealing with these children may seem to require the patience of a saint, and you may not feel all that charitable.

Try to remember that your loss of control will not help matters, and when your child can't control herself, she needs *your* stability. She is comforted by your command of situations and feels very frightened and confused when she sees you lose command.

This is where behavior management techniques come into play. Parents need to learn to react to what the child does in a way that will encourage the repetition of desirable behaviors and discourage those behaviors that are not acceptable. Of course, this is easier said than done, but it is not impossible and can make life much easier.

How to Begin

As we have seen, children with attention deficit vary greatly in their symptoms and in the severity of their deficits. Some of these children behave beautifully at home; their only problems are at school, and many of those problems disappear once the child is diagnosed and begins to receive some special assistance from the teacher. On the other end of the scale, we find the children with ADDH accompanied by conduct disorders, who are extremely difficult to manage and often require professional counseling. In between these are the children with attention deficit who have undesirable behaviors that can be controlled successfully by a behavior management program. Even these in-between children who are helped by such a program are hard to predict. Because of the individual differences of children who have attention deficit, there is no one system that is sure to work for all of them.

Another major problem is that, although a behavior management program is fairly easy to set up, it's very hard to maintain, and eventually you will find some unacceptable behaviors starting to pop up again. Don't panic or think that you have failed; setbacks are to be expected. Acknowledge that your program is no longer working, and determine why. Are you being consistent with enforcement? Have the rewards lost their allure? Modify your program as needed to make it effective again. Or, if necessary, scrap the idea altogether and adopt a new plan. You're not admitting defeat; you're just changing your plan of attack!

What you need is a behavior management program that is uniquely tailored to fit your family's schedule and your child's style. The following section provides you with some sample programs that can be used without alteration or can be fashioned to establish the perfect fit for your child. Perhaps your child will respond well to time-out, grounding, or token economy, exactly as outlined in this chapter. On the other hand, you may need to modify one of these methods or combine techniques from one or more of them.

Don't be afraid or embarrassed to seek the assistance of a professional in setting up your program or in revising it at a later date. This is not an easy task, but it is a very important one that could make a world of difference in the interrelationships of your family members. Get help if you need it—for your child's sake and for your own sake—and never give up!

There are specific situations in which I recommend a highly structured program. Families that are chaotic by nature often need some imposed structure and do well with written rules and firm consequences. Behavioral programs also help structure in some positive reinforcement and give negative parents some practice in positive discipline.

Many families will be able to be much less formal in their discipline. You may not need to put anything in writing or to do much advance planning. Using a great deal of praise and rewarding desirable conduct with video-game, computer, or television time may be all that you need to do in order to keep peace on the home front. Whatever positive approach works for your child and for your family is the right method for you!

Having said all that, let's look at the two main steps involved in developing a structured behavior management program: making the rules and defining the consequences. These steps will require a great deal of communication, cooperation, and consistency, as you begin to lay the foundation for a stronger family structure.

STEP ONE: MAKING THE RULES

The first step is for both parents to work together to set goals for the child and establish a hierarchy of rules. Decide which rule is a necessity, which is important, which would be nice, and which is trivial. For example, it is necessary that your child look both ways before crossing the street, it is important for your child to do her homework, and it would be nice if your child would put her dirty clothes in the clothes hamper. Compliance with the third request would be helpful, but is not essential. Both parents need to agree

on the rules and emphasize those which are necessary or important, learning to overlook and live with the child's less significant
faults.

There must be consistency so that these goals and agreements
do not change from day to day. All children benefit from structure
and dependability, but children with attention deficit have an
added need for stability. They require firm, consistent, and pre-
dictable rules. They need to know that a rule is a rule, no matter
what day it is or which parent is at home.

Children also need to know what the rules mean. Parents
should be very explicit, defining their expectations as simply as
possible. When talking to children about their behavior or giving
them instructions of any kind, there are several important things
to remember. The adult needs to make and maintain eye contact
with the child—it may help to say something like, "Tommy, I need
to see your eyes when I talk to you." The parent should also speak
somewhat more loudly than normal, using a firm voice. Be specific about rules and give definite references to various behaviors,
using physical gestures and demonstrations when appropriate.
Give only one or two instructions at a time, and then have the
child repeat what you have said. In addition, the posting of written
rules around the house may serve as an effective reminder for
children who can read.

STEP TWO:
DEFINING THE CONSEQUENCES
The second step in a behavior management program is to set up
specific punishments for lack of compliance and to clearly explain these to the child. Here again, consistency is the key. "Let
the punishment fit the crime," as Gilbert and Sullivan so aptly
phrased it, and let the punishment be the same every time that
"crime" is committed. Consequences, like rules, should be as
firm and free of surprises as possible.

If undesirable behaviors appear, it is essential that the child is
first given a positive direction encouraging him to pursue a more
acceptable behavior. The use of "No" or "Stop that immediately"
does not redirect the child to a less disruptive task. For example,

if the child is starting to hit her younger sibling, simply yelling at her to stop does not offer a positive approach. On the other hand, interrupting the behavior and suggesting a more positive activity to engage in before the behavior gets out of hand may redirect the child's attention and avoid any more serious confrontation. You might want to grab the closest game and ask the children, "Instead of fighting, don't you think it would be more fun to play this game together?" If the correction is ignored, then an appropriate time-out or other minimal punishment to break the cycle should be instituted. Further deviations should lead to more pronounced disciplinary measures.

In approaching behavior modification techniques, it becomes difficult at times to remember that the child with attention deficit does have a physical problem and that patience is of the essence. This child usually does not intend to misbehave; it's just that his low frustration tolerance, impulsivity, insatiability, and difficulty with changes in routines cause him to have trouble adjusting in many seemingly common circumstances. A parent or other care-taker must be firm, consistent, and also compassionate in understanding the source of the child's problems.

In the following section, I am going to discuss five different types of consequences or disciplinary methods: *physical punishment*, *time-out*, *token economy*, *grounding*, and *natural consequences*. I hope that you will be able to study this information and develop a positive behavior management program which will be helpful for your child.

Different Kinds of Consequences

1. *Physical Punishment.* We want to establish a positive approach with the appropriate reinforcers and incentives. There is very little place for physical punishment in dealing with children who have attention deficit for a number of reasons. First of all, it has very little effect on these children. It has been clearly shown that, although significant punishment in the form of spanking does reverse immediate behavior in most children, they often tend to develop several unwanted side effects, such as more aggressive

behaviors toward others. Children who are spanked usually fail to acquire the desired internal values. Physical punishment also results in more guilt for parents who already feel very guilty.

Of course, physical punishment is undoubtedly needed at times to reverse a significant behavior, especially if there is immediate danger or harm to the child or others around her. Such punishment must always be viewed as a temporary technique to avert danger. We must remember that, in most circumstances, physical punishment is certain to lead to more aggression and acting out behavior.

If spanking doesn't work, what does? Let's take a look at some other disciplinary approaches that may prove much more effective in the long run. (We are not attempting to provide an all-inclusive discussion of these various ideas. It is important, however, to become familiar with the concepts behind these methods of discipline so parents can seek additional help in implementing them.) These approaches can perpetuate family involvement in a positive manner, as well as go a long way to remove the child's lifelong stigma of always doing something wrong.

2. *Time-out.* Basically, this is a method of removing a child from a problem situation and giving him time to cool off and think about what he has done. Time-out is an appropriate disciplinary procedure for children between eighteen months and ten years of age, but is most useful for the younger child. This technique can be instrumental in controlling such problem behaviors as tantrums, biting, hitting, and throwing toys.

Parents need to make several preparations before implementing a time-out program. The most important of these is for both parents to discuss and agree upon the behaviors that will result in time-out. These should be significant offenses.

An appropriate place for the time-out chair must then be selected, and dullness is the key. The chair should be placed in a quiet spot in a hallway or corner where the child cannot see the television or be within reach of toys. The place should not be dark, frightening, or dangerous—just boring. Also, a portable kitchen timer will be needed for enforcement.

It is then time to talk to the child about time-out. Let the child know what behaviors are not acceptable and will necessitate use of the time-out chair. Then explain exactly how time-out works. The child needs to understand that time-out will begin when he is sitting quietly in the chair. If he remains quiet and stays in the chair, he may get up when the timer rings. If he gets out of the chair, you will set him back down and reset the timer. Tell your child that you will be using time-out instead of spanking or yelling. Most children will be glad to learn this, but they will soon realize that they don't like time-out, if it is administered properly. (That is as it should be. You don't want the child to like time-out. You want him to avoid repeating those behaviors that result in the punishment.)

Try a practice run with the child who is old enough. Tell him this is "for pretend." Let him play like he is throwing a toy on the floor. Then tell him very calmly, "You threw a toy, please go to time-out." In this practice session, the child will probably cooperate beautifully. Have him sit quietly for a few seconds before you allow him to get up.

The real thing may not go quite so smoothly. A child who has just "lost it" and has bitten his playmate may not get up obediently and go to sit in the time-out chair. He may, in fact, refuse to go to time-out, or he may even continue his aggressive actions until the parent intervenes.

It is easy for a parent to get angry or start nagging in instances such as these, but that is not what you want to do. Yelling at or reprimanding the child is not appropriate. It is much more effective to use a firm, soft voice and guide the child to the time-out chair as calmly as possible, carrying him if necessary. When you do have to carry the child, hold him facing away from you so he won't confuse what you are doing with a hug.

The timer should be set when the child is sitting in the chair quietly. A maximum of one minute per year of age up to five minutes is suggested. For example, a two-year-old will have two minutes of time-out; a three-year-old, three minutes; and so on. Five minutes should be the maximum time-out, whether the child is five or nine years old. The purpose of time-out is to remove the child from the situation and assure him that you are in control.

Can a two- or three-year-old really understand the concept of time-out? Yes, preschool teachers who work with toddlers daily assure me that time-out works beautifully with that age group. The procedure immediately removes the child from the problem situation and from the other children. No child likes to be isolated and to sit in one place while the other children are playing. A two-year-old, when required to sit in a "Think It Over" chair for a couple of minutes, will benefit from the experience of realizing that she has done something that is unacceptable and that should not be repeated.

Teachers who work with eighteen-month-olds find that a modified version of time-out is effective even with these very young children. When a toddler bites, hits, pushes another down, throws a toy, etc., he is placed in a playpen for a short time. The child would rather be out on the open floor with the other babies and the toys, and he begins to understand that he is denied that privilege when he behaves certain ways.

Timing is essential. When a seven-year-old child gets sassy with a parent, five minutes spent pondering that act in the time-out chair is probably more meaningful than an hour of exile upstairs in her bedroom. After five or ten minutes in her room, the child will forget the original intent of the punishment. The time-out will let the child know that the behavior was not acceptable, but will be short enough that the child can return to the original situation and hopefully do better.

The correction of inappropriate behavior must be immediate. Phrases such as, "Wait till your father gets home," mean nothing to children with attention deficit. It must be remembered that, by delaying consequences and simply repeating expressions of disapproval, a parent tends to feed into a child's need for attention. If the child can gain attention by misbehaving, it is obvious that a parent's continual nagging or scolding will only serve to reward the attention-seeking behavior.

Warnings have no place in a time-out program. They teach the child that he can get away with a transgression one more time. I advise against saying, "If you don't stop that behavior, I'm going to put you in time-out." It is much more effective to put the child in time-out as soon as a significant rule is broken. I recommend that you verbally identify the infraction and initiate the disciplinary procedure immediately. Your child may try to talk you out of it, crying, "But, Mommy, I *forgot.*" Impose the time-out anyway. Give him five minutes to *remember* what type of behavior is and is not acceptable.

When the child's time-out is over, his slate is wiped clean. The parent should not lecture or nag the child about what happened earlier. A brief reminder of the reason for the time-out and a simple suggestion regarding a more acceptable future response for a similar situation should be sufficient. Within a few minutes, the parent should look for good behavior and praise the child accordingly. Like delayed punishment, delayed gratification may be ineffective with children with attention deficit, who need immediate rewards if appropriate conduct is to be reinforced.

When a time-out system fails to work, the parents need to consider several possible reasons. (1) There may be a lack of consistency in enforcement of rules, or it may be that certain adults in charge of the child's discipline are not using the time-out chair at all. (2) Perhaps the child does not get enough attention during the normal course of the day and uses misbehavior to get adults to notice him. It is important for parents to spend a great deal of time noticing their children's good behaviors and giving praise when it is due. (3) The child may not understand the rules. If she doesn't know why she had to go to time-out, she is likely to end up there again for the same reason. (4) Time-out may not seem like such a bad deal. If the chair is in front of a window with a view, if the child can see or hear the television, or if the child is allowed to play with toys or talk to a sibling, the time spent there may be tolerable.

All of these problems can be remedied fairly easily by making some minor adjustments in the enforcement of the program. If you make a diligent attempt to follow the time-out guidelines set forth in this book, you will probably be quite pleased with the results. Be consistent about administering time-out for certain significant behaviors. It will not take long for your child to realize that you mean business and will not tolerate those actions!

3. *Token Economy.* Another type of behavior management technique that you may want to try is the token economy. This type of
program provides for reinforcement of desirable behaviors
through presentation of tokens and punishment of undesirable
conduct by withdrawal of tokens. A home token economy is a
system that allows parents to control and motivate their children's
behavior. This is useful in dealing with older toddlers in a sim-
plified approach, but is usually most appropriate for elementary-
age children.

The first step in setting up a token economy is for the parents to
fill out a contract sheet on which they list desirable behaviors that
will be rewarded and undesirable behaviors that will be fined. The
child should be consulted regarding the listing of privileges that
she can "purchase" with tokens. You might want to consider
allowing as privileges, some of the child's desires that you would
normally not consider, such as staying up late, putting on
makeup, or trying a new hairstyle. After completing the lists of
behaviors and privileges, parents will assign payoffs, fines, and
prices. Some parents even include a contract section in which the
child can fine them for behaviors such as yelling, nagging, or
failing to enforce the economy. This provides an opportunity for
the child to feel that he or she is not the only one being singled
out, but that all family members are working toward more positive
interactions.

Whether you choose to use poker chips, play money, or points
for tokens, you will need to act immediately to reward or punish
certain behaviors. Payoffs and fines should follow close on the
heels of the actions that produce them. There should be no
reason for leniency regarding the administration of the economy.
Rules and consequences should be understood and adhered to.

Nagging should not be necessary. Most parents want their
children to behave appropriately and to do certain chores without
being reminded and scolded. Parents should reward only those
behaviors that occur without verbal prompting—the children will
soon get the idea and initiate their own desirable behaviors.

For a preschool age child, you might want to design a very
simple token economy, working on eliminating one inappropriate

behavior at a time. For example, you could give the child a token of some sort (maybe a sticker on a chart) for sharing toys nicely with his neighbor or for remembering not to hit his sister when they are playing. When the child has earned ten stickers, you could give him a small toy or take him to a movie.

An immediate reward for good behavior that works well with many young children is a picture stamped on the hand. You may want to have several different stamps to use for positive reinforcement. The ink generally stays on the child's hand throughout the day and reminds her of her good conduct. Of course, you may want to comment on the specific action that earned her the reward, so you'll be sure that she remembers and wants to repeat that behavior.

With a child of any age who has a particular problem behavior to work on, a system that documents and rewards successes may be very effective. I have a psychologist friend whose son with attention deficit used to have a terrible time getting ready to go to school in the morning. He would procrastinate with every step of the process, from dressing, to eating, to getting the necessary belongings together. His mother designed a simple morning task chart listing the things that he needed to do every morning. He checked his chores off as he completed them, and he was rewarded at the end of the week if he had done a good job of getting himself ready, without much parental intervention, cheerfully and on time. You might want to use this chart (found on page 120) or modify it to address your own child's weakness.

Robbie enjoyed his morning chore chart and took great pride in his accomplishments. He was the only child in the family who needed this exact type of program, and he didn't want any of his siblings to have one like it. Robbie is now nine years old, and he still checks off his chores every morning. He receives a lot of praise from his parents and grandparents and feels good about that.

If you are able to enforce a home economy the way you and your child have arranged it, you should experience success. Children learn to behave according to their parents' reactions to their behaviors. If you reward desirable behaviors and punish

ROBBIE'S MORNING TASKS

Week of _____

TASK	MON.	TUES.	WED.	THURS.	FRI.
Get dressed					
Eat breakfast					
Brush teeth					
Brush hair					
Get backpack					
Lunch into pack					
Other stuff into pack					
Take medicine					
Take out trash					

(Sydney Paver, Ph.D., Austin Mental Health Associates)

undesirable ones, you should succeed in molding your child's behavior.

4. *Grounding.* A disciplinary technique that can have long-term positive effects on a child's behavior is grounding. This method teaches a child the consequences of improper conduct, while at the same time providing your child with instruction regarding various household chores. Used most frequently with children who are eight years or older, grounding is designed for those who can read and perform housekeeping tasks. It also works well with older school-age children.

Grounding is a simple process that requires a minimum of preparation on the parents' part. First of all, as with time-out, the parents must agree on the rules and determine what infractions are punishable by this method. Again, these behavioral offenses must be specific and significant. For example, a tense parent should not overreact and ground a child for something relatively insignificant.

Secondly, the parents and child need to sit down together and develop a list of ten jobs that the child is capable of doing around the house and that are not included among the child's regular, required chores. These jobs should be comparable in difficulty and in the amount of time required for completion—such as sweeping and mopping the kitchen, cleaning the bathroom, and raking the yard.

Each chore should be recorded on an index card with a detailed description of all parts of the task. You should explain to your child that she will be assigned a certain number of job cards when she breaks an important rule, for example, when she lies about having homework to do. The child will randomly pull the assigned number of job cards from the file box and will be grounded until those chores have been completed.

While the child is grounded, she must attend school, perform the required tasks, and follow the house rules. This usually means that the child must stay in her room unless she is working, eating, or attending school. All of the following entertainments are prohibited: television, stereo, telephone calls, and games. Social activities, including visits from friends, are forbidden as well.

The child is grounded until the jobs are completed satisfactorily. Parents should check to be sure that all parts of all chores have been adequately executed. If the chores have been done correctly, you should praise your child and end the grounding. If a job requires more work, let your child know exactly what she needs to do in order to become "ungrounded."

Your child is actually determining how long she is being grounded. The grounding may take fifteen minutes or two days. If the grounding seems to be taking an unusually long time, check to be sure that your child's life is dull enough and that you are not giving the child a lot of attention.

You will know that grounding has been effective when your child becomes more aware of the consequences of breaking rules and begins to do a better job of following your guidelines. Then you may be doing your own housework again, but it will be well worth it.

5. *Natural consequences.* We should note here that consequences need not always be imposed by the parents. There are natural consequences that will follow many instances of misconduct. Some examples of these are tiredness after staying up too late or being very cold after refusing to put on a coat. Of course, you want to be sure that the natural consequence poses no danger to the child. You may mention the natural consequence in a matter-of-fact manner. If the child still refuses to cooperate and the consequences are not dangerous, letting these results evolve instead of creating a scene may be appropriate. A safe natural consequence, in many cases, will serve as an effective punishment. Children will "learn their lesson" without being nagged or punished by their parents.

For instance, let's say that your ten-year-old daughter takes her five dollars of birthday money on an outing to the beach. She wants to spend the entire amount for two $2.49 stuffed animals at the first souvenir shop that you visit. You could say, "No," if you think the toys are a waste of money, or you could tell her that she can buy one of the animals, but she has to save the rest of her money. A better option might be to teach her a lesson. Since it's her money, tell her it's her decision. But you can point out benefits and consequences. Say, "If you just buy one of the animals now, you'll have money left to buy something else nice later."

This may be a very hard lesson for an insatiable child with attention deficit to learn. When she sees something that she wants, she desires it desperately—right then! It's likely that she will choose to go on and get it. Then she'll see something else that she wants just as badly later on. She will beg you to advance her some money. She'll promise to pick up all 176 things that are on the floor of her room the minute she gets home if you'll get it for her. If you refuse, she'll say you don't trust her.

This is your big chance to teach her an important lesson. Don't give in—even if you desperately want those 176 items picked up! Be kind and understanding, but be firm. Let her know that it is good to spend wisely. You may need to repeat this scenario many times. You can't expect this kind of lesson to be learned readily.

Hopefully, the idea will sink in eventually. The important thing is that you have given your child some responsibility and some experience in decision making.

Points to Remember

Methods of praise and criticism are of utmost importance. Parents should neither praise nor criticize a child as a whole person. Comment on a specific act instead, making it very clear what the child did to incur your approval or disapproval. If you simply say, "What a good girl!" or "You were a bad boy today," the child may not know what she or he did to "earn" the label.

Since children with attention deficit feel that they rarely live up to adults' expectations, it is important for parents to be on the lookout for times to praise. Don't wait for perfection. Praise the child for attempting to complete a task or for improving in some way. You could say, "I like the way you are putting your toys away," or "I'm proud of you for making a better grade on this week's spelling test."

When a child does something wrong, tell him what you don't like and what you would prefer that he do the next time. For example, you might say, "I am unhappy that you yelled at your sister to 'shut up.' I'd like for you to say, 'Please be quiet,' next time."

Whether you choose to implement time-out, grounding, token economy, a combination of these disciplines, or another method altogether, it will soon become obvious that some behaviors cannot be adequately anticipated and thus discussed with the child beforehand. It is hard to make all the rules in anticipation of all the infractions. However, with these general approaches and a consistent but positive manner, interpretation from one act to the next can take place. If a child knows that he is expected to wash his face first thing in the morning, the same approach can easily be applied to brushing of his teeth.

Another key point to keep in mind in designing any behavior strategy is that, even with the best-behaved child, not all behaviors can be legislated. For example, it is clearly important for a child to understand that she is not to strike her younger sibling. On the other hand if she takes the sibling's toy, that's a situation that can probably be settled with some gentle conversation. Parents should try to target only those behaviors that are disruptive and difficult to deal with. Constant harping on minor annoyances will only frustrate the child and perpetuate a lack of self-esteem.

It is also important to have some degree of flexibility. I think it is possible to be flexible and consistent at the same time, and I'll give you some examples. You have had a really hard day at work, and your kids have been arguing ever since you picked them up at school. You are frantically trying to get dinner on the table so you won't be late to your son's soccer game, when he pushes his brother off the couch and a fight ensues. Having had about as much as you can stand, you yell "I want both of you to go to your rooms right now! You can stay there till you're thirty-five!" Naturally, when everything calms down and you have time to evaluate the situation, you realize that you lost your temper and were unreasonable in your handling of the situation. You need to be able to go to your kids and tell them that you have thought about the consequences and realize that you need to change their punishment. In an incident like the one described above, by the time you cool off, you may decide that your child has been isolated long enough. Other situations may be different, depending on your child's age and the severity of the offense. You won't remove the consequences; you'll just make any alterations that seem appropriate once you are thinking more objectively.

I would also recommend using some flexibility when it will help in encouraging your child to use self-control. Many children with attention difficulties have trouble controlling themselves, due to their impulsivity and social immaturity. Medication can help in this area, as we have seen, but it is important for these children to get some grip on their emotions. Many of these kids cannot handle being punished and become utterly hysterical when they are sent to time-out or are told that they are being grounded. It may help for your child to know that you will be flexible regarding his punishment. When he breaks a significant rule, he will be punished immediately, every time, without question—there's your consistency. If he can control himself and accept his punishment, however, you will cut the punishment in half. For example, he will only have half of the time-out or will only lose half as much television or video-game time. On the other hand, if the kid yells and screams and totally loses control of himself, you will enforce the punishment.

When you start using this system to improve your child's self-control, you may want to be extra flexible. Remember that it's very hard for your child to manage his emotions. If you work with him on this, it is likely that you will see some results. Once your child understands that it will always be this way, he will probably begin to develop some self-control that will carry over into other situations. The more control he has, the better your child will feel.

Children need to feel responsible for and capable of controlling themselves. Parents can help by telling children that everyone has trouble with self-control. Tell your children that even you lose your temper sometimes. Assure your child that he *can* keep from hitting his sister. He needs to hold his breath, count to ten, or hit a pillow. Help your child make games for finding ways to control himself. The child with attention deficit needs to learn that self-control is possible and is desirable.

It must be remembered and emphasized repeatedly that firmness does not replace compassion, which children with attention deficit need as much as anyone else. Some families can get so involved with behavioral techniques that they forget to recognize the child's feelings. Sometimes, a parent needs to hug a child and say, "You must feel it's hard for an eight-year-old to control her behavior all the time. I'll bet you were very angry when I asked you to sit in time-out."

There are also times when the parent needs to help the child socially. Since children with attention deficit are typically socially immature, they often have trouble with peer relationships. They may prefer the company of older or younger children (or of adults), because children their own age may not tolerate their actions. Parents may need to invite their child's peers over to play where their child has the "home court" advantage. The parents can then observe what is going on and "take notes"; if they notice particular areas of their child's socialization that need work, they can work on these later.

Social coaching can prove invaluable to the child who has attention difficulties. Parents can impart social skills through counseling or role play. They can encourage their children to plan out how they will act when presented with certain social situations. For example, the child can practice approaching other children and entering into conversation, as well as working on verbal responses for various situations. If the child is called a nerd, for instance, he can have a standard reply of, "My name is Tommy, not Nerd."

Of course, it is impossible to anticipate every problem and to have an answer or a proposed plan of action for every social circumstance. Every child, even with the best of coaching from home, is going to experience some difficulties with peers. When a child is upset after having a social problem, the parent needs to be a listening ear—not a judge. The parent doesn't have to offer the solution to the problem. Your child may need a sympathetic ear more than he needs a critique on his behavior or advice about what he should do. Allow him to come up with his own solutions and changes in behavior by talking about the problem later. For example, the next day ask your child, "Did you think about what happened on the way home from school? Do you know what you will do about it if it happens again, or how you will keep it from happening again?"

Many schools and psychologists offer peer group counseling, in which children practice social skills in small groups with children their age. Behavioral change techniques are used to promote problem-solving skills, self-control, responsibility, self-confidence, and general socialization. The primary goals of these socialization groups involve teaching children how to do the following: make and keep friends, solve problems instead of complaining, handle fearful situations, express unhappiness verbally, take action to produce happy feelings, follow instructions, reduce lying, eliminate stealing, deal with name calling, and be an effective leader. Children have the opportunity to learn and practice skills with peers in a safe and supportive environment. Feedback sessions with parents are used to establish goals for the individual children and to discuss behavior management approaches that can be used in the home.

Like other children, the child with attention deficit needs freedom and encouragement to express ideas and feelings, understanding, nurturance, and, above all, love. It is essential for this child to feel needed. She may experience more failure and discouragement than the average child, and it will enhance her self-esteem if she knows that she is needed in the home. Make her responsible for doing or helping with certain chores at which she can be successful, like putting away her clean laundry in her drawers or assisting Dad in washing the car. It will help immeasurably for your child to know that she has certain responsibilities that help the household run smoothly. Tell her frequently how very important she is to you and how much you love her. A shortage of love and understanding will render any behavior modification technique useless as far as helping a child develop positive self-esteem and self-control at the same time. The earlier that these interventions can take place, the more success that can be achieved for both the parents and the child.

THE OTHER FAMILY MEMBERS

The child with attention deficit may require a great deal of your time and energy, and this may cause problems with other children in the family. The siblings of this child need your support and nurturing as well. When they are old enough to understand what is going on, explain attention deficit to them and let them know why their sibling needs some special help. Tell them that concentration and self-control are very hard for this sibling and that he needs assistance in these areas. You might even want to put the siblings on the same program that the other child is on, just so they won't feel left out. Or there may be a special way that you can give some extra attention to these children to make up for all the extra time you are spending with the child who has attention deficit. Be sure your other children know how much you love them and appreciate their understanding.

Summary

Parents must avoid reinforcing negative behaviors as much as possible. You can begin by ignoring the silly, inappropriate behaviors and by establishing firm, consistent, but fair consequences for the more severe misconduct. As usual, your responses should be, as much as possible, established prior to the altercations. These responses must be consistent and immediate to be effective when you are attempting to alter specific behavioral patterns. A quiet, calm approach to handling the child's behavioral infractions is essential.

Appropriate incentives should also be introduced, offering significant rewards that a child can work toward in improving specific behaviors. Frequently, these programs can be discussed with your pediatrician and be set up as a team. At other times, perhaps more extensive collaboration with a psychologist would be helpful. It should be remembered that each of these approaches must be varied somewhat, depending on the age of the child. Although time-out may be successful with a five- or six-year-old, this obviously would not work for an adolescent, who may need to have certain privileges restricted.

Most importantly, parents must keep in mind that behavior management is not going to be easy—either for you or for your child. It is not likely that one approach will work indefinitely. Modify your method, or try a new one, if necessary. Seek the support and understanding that professionals can offer, and do your best to provide sympathy for your children. The more diligent you are at following these guidelines, the more successful and satisfying the entire situation will become.

9.

The School's Role in Treating Attention Difficulties

Frowny-faced stickers, red-inked teachers' notes about messy or late papers, and time-outs for talking or getting out of their seats too much—all are everyday classroom occurrences for children with attention difficulties. Lectures, reading assignments, and study sheets that require much sustained attention are beyond the realm of possibility for these students. They either drift off into a world of daydreams or distract others by fidgeting and talking to their neighbors.

Since much of the frustration and failure that these young people encounter is in the classroom, the educational aspect becomes an essential part of the treatment. It's imperative to treat the whole child; a strong alliance between physician, parent, and school will reap significant dividends in the child's overall remediation process.

What can you do as a parent to ensure that school is a positive experience for your child? You must become involved in the educational process and take an active part on behalf of your child's education.

If You *Think* Your Child May Have Attention Deficit

If you suspect your child may be having attention difficulties, schedule a conference with the teacher early in the school year.

Give the instructor detailed information substantiating your theory, and request that the teacher observe your child carefully and give you some feedback. If the teacher is not familiar with attention deficit, you may need to supply some information on the topic.

Also let the teacher know that you want your child to be formally evaluated. Schools cannot diagnose attention deficit, but counselors can administer IQ tests and several other procedures that are part of the standard evaluation. The school's testing is free of charge and will save money on your doctor bill.

When You *Know* Your Child Has Attention Deficit

If your child has already been diagnosed as having attention deficit, talk to the principal in August and request a teacher who is experienced in dealing with these children. Arrange a conference with the teacher during the first few weeks of school and share all pertinent information regarding your child's style of learning. You probably know better than anyone else what motivational and disciplinary methods work best with your child. You are in a position to provide the teacher with priceless information that will make his or her job much easier and will improve your child's chances for a positive learning experience.

It will be important for you to discuss your child's therapy with the teacher. If the child is on medication, ask the instructor to let you know if the dosage seems appropriate. When a child who takes medication for attention deficit cannot concentrate well enough to get his work done or is hyperactive, his dosage is probably too low. On the other hand, if the child is chronically lethargic or drowsy at school after getting plenty of sleep at night, it is likely that the dosage of medication is too high. As the year goes on and your child grows in weight and stature, the dosage may need to be increased. The teacher will probably be the best judge of this need, based on your child's ability, or inability, to concentrate on his schoolwork. Of course, anxieties in the child's life such as family stress and difficulties with peers or siblings can bring on sudden behavioral changes that may be totally independent of any medication effects. It is thus essential to have a cooperative effort between teacher, parent, and physician, which should make the regulation of the medication a much more precise science.

How to Survive a Parent/Teacher Conference

For all the reasons outlined above, you will naturally want to maintain contact with your child's teacher throughout the school year. Sometimes notes and phone calls will suffice. But there will be times when more lengthy conferences will be necessary. You will need to make an appointment with the teacher, and it is perfectly acceptable to request that other individuals who work with your child, instructors or counselors, for example, be present as well.

Preparing yourself mentally and emotionally for a conference is always advisable. It will be helpful for you to make notes in advance about your questions and concerns. You might want to ask your child if she has questions or particular problems about which you should ask the instructor. This is a good way to involve the child in her own education and let her know that her ideas and feelings are important.

If any of the questions involves a serious problem or situation that provokes your anger, it will be worthwhile for you to work at dispelling your irritation prior to the meeting. It will be hard for you to benefit from what is being said if you are angry or tense. You also need to try to be objective, remembering that people's viewpoints differ and that there are usually at least two sides to every story.

When you are conferring with educational professionals (or medical personnel, for that matter), feel free to ask a lot of questions. If terminology is used that you don't understand, request an explanation. Professionals become accustomed to referring to behaviors, educational and psychological methods, learning disabilities, and other disorders in technical terms and they sometimes forget to clarify their statements for parents. Most of these people really want you to understand what they are saying and will be glad to answer your questions.

If Necessary, Going Elsewhere for Help

I want to emphasize that, in the vast majority of cases, teachers are sensitive to the problems of children who have attention difficulties and are more than willing to help. Their assistance is invaluable, due to the amount of time they spend working with your child in school.

Unfortunately, however, the time may come when you will follow every suggestion outlined above and still receive no satisfaction whatsoever. You may then need to talk to someone with more authority. It is never pleasant to go over someone's head or to risk being viewed as a "complainer," but your child's well-being is at stake.

For example, let's say that your son is doing poorly in second grade. He fails to finish most of his assignments, and some of the ones he does complete get lost before he turns them in. He can answer the teacher's questions orally, but he has great difficulty putting anything down on paper. His handwriting is messy, and his spelling is atrocious. And in spite of all his problems, it is apparent to all adults who work with him that he is extremely intelligent.

You, the parent, after reading this book, suspect that your son has attention deficit. You know that there are a number of other possibilities that could have the same manifestations and need to be ruled out, of course, and you want to have the child tested.

The teacher, on the other hand, strongly disagrees with your hypothesis and refuses to refer your child for testing. She says that your son is just lazy, that he isn't trying. Since, on some occasions, your son turns in excellent papers *on time*, the teacher insists that the child is capable of doing whatever he wants to do. He obviously has an attitude problem.

What is a parent to do? Tell the teacher that you need to discuss this problem with someone at the school who has more information and make an appointment to talk to the coordinator of the school's special education program, or a school counselor. If that individual is unable or unwilling to help, make it clear that you will need to talk to the principal.

In attempting to negotiate the system, on rare occasions you may eventually end up on the doorstep of the Special Education Director or even the superintendent of the school district. Hopefully, however, your search for assistance will not need to go that far. If you are lucky, as most of us are, your child's teacher will be like many of today's educators—sensitive to students' individual differences and happy to do whatever is necessary to help these children achieve according to their potential.

Remember, however, at any point in the educational process, that you can turn to your physician for help. If he or she is not experienced in dealing with learning or attention problems, ask for a referral to someone who can be of more assistance.

Resource Help for Children with Learning Problems

No matter what happens, do not give up on your endeavors to get to the root of your child's problem. There is a great deal of help available for children with learning problems, once they are officially diagnosed. If there is a significant discrepancy between a child's academic achievement and her intellectual capabilities in certain areas—oral or written expression, listening or reading comprehension, reading skills, spelling, or mathematical calculation and reasoning—then the child is considered "learning disabled." This does not mean that the child is "mentally retarded." It simply means that she is unable to perform in accordance with her intellectual potential. This "learning disabled" designation qualifies students for special assistance from resource teachers who have been trained to help these children compensate for their problems.

Of course, not all children with attention deficit have learning disabilities, and many of these students will not be eligible for resource help. In many school districts ADD is a diagnosis that does not qualify a child for special assistance. Because of their concentration problems, however, these students may need the help of resource personnel in order to succeed academically. Students with attention deficit often make much greater strides when social and academic successes are encouraged within a smaller group. A more intimate setting can also provide the support and emotional warmth that are obviously valuable but are often lacking within a large group.

In some school districts, students with attention deficit can qualify for the special education program based upon a physician's recommendation. Placing your child in one of these programs, if the teachers and doctor think it is advisable, can only help your child.

Sometimes students who have attention deficit require a very small amount of special assistance. Depending on their needs, these students may spend just thirty minutes or an hour a day in the resource room, getting help with their assignments and learning special coping techniques. They then return to the normal classroom and continue to do the same work the other students are doing.

Other students with attention deficit may have such severe learning, behavioral, or emotional problems that they may need special help throughout the day. These children may spend the entire day in the resource room, and, in some school districts, they may even be sent to special schools. With the concerted, caring effort put forth by specially trained instructors, and with the proper support from family and physicians, these students may experience marked improvement, both academically and socially, and eventually be placed back in the regular classroom.

Unfortunately, though, in some areas, due to lack of funding, a very fine line is drawn that denies this assistance to the student who has attention deficit. If you feel that your child needs extra help, and if that aid is not available through the school system, you might want to look for a private tutor who is knowledgeable regarding concentration problems. Your child's teacher, counselor, or physician might be able to recommend someone who works with children who have attention deficit disorder.

There is a good possibility, of course, that your child will not need any resource help. Many students with attention deficit, on appropriate medication, if needed, and with the support of caring physicians, parents, and instructors, will show dramatic improvements in the areas of academics, conduct, and social skills.

As we have seen, no two children who have attention difficulties are exactly alike. These individuals experience varying types and degrees of difficulty, and their needs, therefore, differ accordingly. It is essential that parents own up to the fact that their children have attention deficit. You must first be able to admit to yourself that your child has a problem—then you must have the courage to share that admission with the professionals who can help your child. This becomes particularly difficult in the school setting, where you may feel some initial embarrassment regarding your child's need for special assistance. You don't want your child to be labeled as "retarded" or "dumb" and you may even want your child to be in the Talented and Gifted (TAG) program—not in Special Education. Many parents refuse to have their children placed in the classes that can help their children the most, and frequently, the stigma is only in the parents' minds. A mother recently told me that she overheard her daughter with attention deficit give the following response to a friend who had just announced that she had been selected for TAG: "Well, I've been selected for resource!" Children are rarely embarrassed to go to resource classes. The resource teachers are often outstanding and offer tempting rewards as reinforcements. Resource classes sometimes have special celebrations or go on special field trips. Although some students may be teased because they go to the resource room, they generally have a positive experience there and occasionally find that someone who teases them is jealous.

I would urge you to cooperate with the school and take advantage of all assistance that is available for your child. Sometimes, a child on a treatment plan that incorporates medical, psychological, and educational approaches will improve greatly in every area—he may even become eligible for that Talented and Gifted program. Only when you are able to admit that your child has different needs, and only when you are willing to seek the help that your child deserves, will that child have a chance at developing concentration skills.

Should Your Child Repeat a Grade?

This is another important and emotional question that you may have to face as the parent of a child with learning problems— especially if those problems have not been professionally evaluated and treated. It is not uncommon these days for teachers to suggest that certain students should be retained in kindergarten or first grade, in the hope that added maturity and skills will improve the child's academic performance.

If a teacher recommends holding your child back in school, be sure to carefully weigh all the possibilities and ramifications. This may be the point at which some testing should be done to determine the true nature of your child's problems.

When young age and/or immaturity are found to be the *major* culprits, then your child may benefit greatly from another year in kindergarten or first grade. For the young student who has significant difficulties with fine motor skills like printing, drawing, and cutting, or simply with adjusting to school routine and being separated from his or her parents, an added year of development may be ideal.

But if your child has learning disabilities or attention deficit, it is unlikely that retention would be particularly helpful; it could even make matters worse. For one thing, social immaturity is a characteristic of attention deficit, and your child may be more than one year behind in his level of maturity. When he repeats kindergarten, he still may not be as mature as the students who are a year younger than he is. The reason that the child is not doing well in school is that he can't focus, not because he is immature. Although he may fit in better socially with a younger group of children, he will probably still have trouble concentrating, and may even have more trouble concentrating, if he repeats a grade, due to boredom.

Schools avoid the use of the word "failure" in regard to retention these days, but the child still experiences the disappointment of not being promoted with his friends. Children who have attention deficit with all their other problems, do not need that added psychological burden and may not benefit from repeating the grade anyway.

You should also consider the unpleasant possibility that, at some point farther down the line, a child with learning or attention problems may fail to make passing grades. Of course, this is not likely to happen if the student is receiving the proper medical, behavioral, and educational therapy. However, should your child actually "fail" one of the upper grades, you might regret that earlier elective retention, since he will end up two years behind in school.

Whether or not to retain a child in a particular grade is an important decision that should be made with great care by parents, teacher, counselor, and possibly a physician.

Conquering Homework

Seeing that your child with attention deficit gets her homework done may be one of your most miraculous feats as a parent. Your child doesn't want to do homework—very few children do. The child with attention deficit is even more strongly opposed to the idea than her peers who do not have this problem—after a mentally and emotionally exhausting day at school, more paperwork is the last thing she's interested in. She wants to play, watch TV, or just rest. As much as she needs a break, the homework must be done, since she will probably be receiving a grade for it.

So, first of all, give your child that break she needs when she gets home from school. It sounds great to have a rule that the child cannot play or watch television until she gets her homework done, but that type of regulation may not be practical for the child with attention deficit. In addition, other breaks will be needed once the homework is begun. Consider your child's age and attention span and do whatever works best for her. For example, with a third

grader, you might want to try a half-hour break after school with a
ten-minute break after every fifth math problem. Try using a timer
and offering small incentives for your child to return to her desk
cheerfully.

Setting is all-important: your child needs a quiet, well-lit work
place. It needs to be in an area that is free of distractions, far away
from the noise of television, radio, stereo, or voices. It would probably help if the child were not facing a window or anything else of
interest. Be sure that your child has all the supplies she needs—
books, paper, pencil, pencil sharpener, eraser, and pen. Then she
won't have the "I didn't have my _____ " excuse for getting up.

At times, you may need to sit with your child and give her some
one-on-one assistance. This may be the hardest part of the whole
ordeal since it's easy to get impatient and frustrated when working
with an uncooperative child, but it's important not to lose your
temper and give up. Let your child know that you are in control
and that she must comply. Occasionally, you might want to make
an exception and let your child experience the "natural consequences" of not doing her homework—whether those consequences mean making a low grade, having to miss recess to do
the work, or failing an unstudied-for test. Sometimes those consequences will prove more effective than whatever you might do at
home.

Working with your child may also prove difficult because of the
modern ways of working math problems or labeling parts of
speech. If your way of arriving at common denominators or doing
long division is not the "right" way, because it's not the way Miss
Adams says to do it, you may get into some trouble. You may need
to arrange a conference with the teacher so you can learn the new
methods and figure out what your child is supposed to be doing.

When your child knows what to do and doesn't need your
assistance, it's best for him to work independently—if he will.
You might just discuss the assignment with him briefly to begin
with and watch him do the first problem or answer the first
question for "practice." When he finishes the paper, I would
suggest that you check it to be sure that problems are copied
correctly and that no careless errors have been made. You may

find that your child doesn't understand the work as well as he thinks he does, and you may be in a position to help. Your aid in getting mistakes corrected may prove invaluable. Your child can learn a lot more from your explanations than he can from a returned paper with red "X" marks on it.

If your child has been diagnosed as having attention deficit and takes medication during the school day, you have the priceless option of giving your child a low dose of medication after school so he can concentrate on his homework. As I emphasized in Chapter Seven, if the medication makes the school day much easier, don't be afraid to give an additional dose after school. You will need to give your child the medicine as soon as he gets home, and then let him have a break until the medicine takes effect—approximately thirty minutes. With the benefit of the medication, your child will be able to concentrate at least as well as most of his peers, and he will probably be relatively cooperative and easy to work with. The medication may go a long way toward reducing frustration and power struggles over the completion of homework.

You really don't need to worry about this after-school medication upsetting your child's daily dosage. If your child has homework or music lessons every day after school and regularly needs the help of medication, your physician will simply space the recommended dosage throughout the day and prescribe the amount to be taken daily after school. Many children, particularly those in the earlier elementary grades, have homework only occasionally; but those occasions can become nightmares, due to the child's inability to focus and his fatigue after a long day at school. I would encourage you to give your child a low dose of medication at those times, with your doctor's approval. Usually, a small extra dose after school will have no adverse effect on a child's overall treatment program.

Communication with the School

Parent/teacher communication is a key ingredient of academic success for a student who is experiencing attention difficulties.

There is so much important information regarding your child's background that will prove invaluable to the instructor. And as the year progresses, you will want to let the teacher know about any stress your child is experiencing—whether it is related to the family situation, peer relationships, or school itself. It may even help the teacher to know that your child got up on the wrong side of the bed this morning or didn't feel well over the weekend.

Send notes to the teacher and request telephone or in-person conferences when necessary. Take every opportunity to help your child by keeping the teacher in the know. Don't leave educators guessing. They are in a much better position to help your child when they understand what is going on in his life.

Ask your child daily if he has brought home any notes from teachers or if there is anything special going on at school. You can help your child immeasurably by staying on top of her school schedule and helping her remember "special dress" days, Show and Tell, library day, picture day, and so on.

You might want to check frequently to see if your child has adequate supplies at school or if there is anything special that he should be taking to school with him that day. When school starts at 7:50 A.M., your child will invariably tell you at 7:35 that he is out of notebook paper, needs a new spiral, or has lost his scissors. What's worse, he will give you two minutes' warning on needing an empty toilet paper roll, a picture of an animal's home, or a costume for the class play. Perhaps some prodding on your part the day before might have elicited these responses and given you a little more preparation time!

By communicating frequently with your child about school and with the school about your child, you will be doing everyone involved a great service! Most importantly, you will be doing your part in seeing that your child has a positive learning experience.

Annual Review
of School Records

The National Committee for Citizens in Education recommends that parents of public school students schedule an appointment every spring to review their children's confidential school records. Spring is a good time for using test scores and samples of the year's schoolwork to plan for the next year. It is also the time for striking from the record all outdated comments regarding your child's behavior.

The Family Educational Rights and Privacy Act of 1974 gives parents the right to do the following: inspect records within forty-five days of your request; see all records pertaining to your child, including those in computer files, on microfiche, or in folders; ask that records be corrected or deleted if they are inaccurate, inappropriate, misleading, or in violation of privacy; have someone interpret test scores or other information that you do not understand; and provide or withhold written consent for the release of records to anyone outside the school system.

Summary

As we have seen, there is much that parents and physicians can accomplish when serving as advocates for the child who has attention deficit. By working with the school and sharing all pertinent information regarding your child with teachers and counselors, you can take an active part in your child's education. By cooperating with school personnel and allowing your child to have the advantage of all resources that are available, you will be ensuring that your child gets the best education possible.

10.

The Teacher's Role in Treating Attention Difficulties

As we have seen, there is much that the parent and physician can accomplish when serving as advocates for the child with attention deficit. The person in the best position to assure that child of a positive learning experience, however, is the classroom teacher. For that reason, this chapter will be devoted to suggestions for educators. (Parents need to keep reading, though, just in case your child's teacher misses this!)

First of all, America's teachers and school systems have recently been criticized for asking doctors to "drug" problem students in order to make classrooms more manageable. Such accusations are infuriating and frustrating beyond belief to responsible educators and physicians who are doing everything within their power to help students who have attention deficit concentrate, learn, and feel good about themselves. With appropriate diagnosis and treatment, these children are likely to experience a wonderful turnabout that can change their lives.

Recognizing Hyperactive ADD Students

Considering the prevalence of attention deficit, which we discussed earlier, it is likely that there will be at least one of these students in every classroom. The ones who are hyperactive, and those who have conduct disorders as well, should be very easy to spot.

Hyperactive students rarely sit still. They are continually getting up from their desks to look for supplies, borrow things, ask questions, and complain about other students. Even when they stay in their seats, these children are in motion, shuffling their feet, scratching, tapping their pencils, and twirling their hair. In short, they fidget endlessly.

On the playground, the hyperactive child may move from one activity or skirmish to another. Due to his impulsivity, he may get hurt more frequently than other children because he doesn't think before acting.

Children with conduct disorders are also standouts, since they have so much trouble following classroom rules and interacting with others in an appropriate manner. These students have a very low boiling point and tend to "erupt" when they become frustrated. They may be frequent occupants of the time-out chair or visitors to the principal's office.

Teachers shouldn't hesitate about talking to the parents of hyperactive students and letting them know that there could be a physiological cause for their children's behavior. These parents have probably struggled through years of anguish and frustration with these children and probably harbor a deep sense of guilt. The idea that this could be a physiological problem with possibilities for successful treatment will be more than a welcome relief to these parents; it will be an offer of hope for a new life for the child and family.

Spotting Students with Attention Problems in Early Elementary School

As we saw in the earlier chapters, children with attention deficit and without hyperactivity are the hardest ones to spot. If teachers and counselors don't spot these children, it's quite possible that no one will. These youngsters are often bright and easy to get along with. They do well within the family structure and show no real signs of being different until they start school.

Since most children with attention deficit are not hyperactive, it follows that teachers will encounter many more children with simple attention deficit than those with the more obvious characteristic of hyperactivity. What should the teacher look for when considering the possibility of attention deficit? I discussed these characteristics in great detail in Chapter Two, and teachers of young elementary school children will find a lot of valuable information in Chapter Five.

In review, the primary characteristics that will show up in the early elementary classroom are distractibility (especially within a group), free flight of ideas, occasional impulsivity, lack of organization, inability to complete classroom tasks, poor short-term memory, and often social immaturity. Children with attention deficit generally fail to live up academically to their intellectual potential. Of course, there can be many reasons for this, but a knowledgeable teacher who has any reason to suspect attention deficit or learning disabilities has everything to gain from suggesting to the parents that the child be tested.

An Intervention
with a Happy Ending

The following success story of a teacher's intervention will serve as a helpful illustration. Katy, a funny, bright, and happy little girl had a sky-high self-concept before she started kindergarten. With an August 28 birthday, and living in a school district that required children to be five years old before September 1 to begin kindergarten, Katy started school on August 22 at age four. She was the youngest child in her class, and, being very short for her age, was also the smallest.

Unfortunately, Katy's young age and social immaturity were logical scapegoats for many of the problems that she was to encounter in school. Difficulties in conduct and study habits were the main concerns at first, but Katy's primary problem was her talkativeness. She had something to say about everything and tended to call out answers without getting permission. During naptime, when Katy was supposed to rest quietly for forty-five minutes, she couldn't keep silent or still for long.

Academics per se posed only minor problems for Katy in kindergarten. She had mastered many of the school district's language and math objectives for kindergartners by the age of three or four. Her greatest difficulty was in "staying on task" to finish papers. She would get started on a project and then start daydreaming or looking around at everything else that was going on in the room. Katy frequently had trouble with multistepped directions—she might follow one instruction and then have no idea what to do next. Her report cards always indicated that she needed improvement in the areas of listening, following directions, staying on task, and demonstrating an adequate attention span for her age.

Despite Katy's problems, the teacher considered her delightful and felt that all of these difficulties were due to immaturity. Although having a student repeat kindergarten is a fairly common practice when the child needs the benefit of an added year of maturity, the teacher felt that this was inadvisable in Katy's case. Because of Katy's intelligence, her teacher felt that a second year in kindergarten would only bore Katy and compound her problems, so she recommended some structured summer activities for Katy while promoting her to the first grade.

Of course, first grade was a year of "serious business" and posed all the same problems that Katy had experienced in kindergarten, but to a much greater degree. It seemed like Katy was always in trouble. Her name was continually on the board for talking without permission or for failing to finish assignments on time. She had to stay after school several days a week to finish papers, and she had her grades lowered for lateness and for forgetting to put her name on her work.

Sometimes, however, Katy did very well on her assignments, leading her teacher to believe that Katy was quite capable of doing anything she wanted to do. The instructor felt that this was simply a matter of attitude or lack of motivation, but, even after trying every trick in the book, the teacher had very little success in consistently motivating Katy to get her act together.

The teacher was very fond of Katy, finding her extremely creative, and she fully expected Katy to grow up to be quite successful in some artistic endeavor, but she didn't know what to do with her in the meantime. This instructor, like the kindergarten teacher, blamed Katy's immaturity for her problems and felt that, once the maturity came along, Katy would be a straight-A student. This first grade teacher, too, thought that retention would be a major mistake.

So Katy entered second grade, and, unfortunately, the maturity still wasn't there. Katy's grades were satisfactory, but certainly not in keeping with her intelligence. Her report cards, as before, consistently indicated a need for improvement in completing work on time, listening effectively, following directions, and obeying school rules.

The second-grade teacher loved Katy. After observing her carefully and trying one method after another to keep her on task and "bring her back" from daydreams, this teacher concluded that Katy's problem had nothing to do with attitude or lack of motivation. Katy really seemed to be trying her very hardest, but she just couldn't concentrate, no matter how hard she tried.

The teacher told her own father, a psychiatrist, all about Katy. He gave her medical journal articles and attention deficit checklists. After some research and careful consideration, the instructor shared this information with Katy's parents.

The teacher went over a list of attention deficit characteristics with the parents, discussing each one in relation to Katy's academic and behavioral performance at school. Many of the characteristics (hyperactivity, in particular) didn't apply to Katy at all, but the most important ones (distractibility, short attention span, and impulsivity) described the child's difficulties perfectly. Katy's parents were enthusiastic about having her tested.

School counselors evaluated Katy and found her to have an above-average IQ with notable discrepancies between her intellectual capabilities and her performance. Except in the area of spelling, however, these discrepancies were not significant enough to indicate learning disabilities or to qualify Katy for resource assistance. The counselors did, however, note Katy's distractibility and impulsivity during time-consuming tests. Based upon this observation and the teacher's detailed reports, the school referred Katy to my clinic for further assessment.

A neurodevelopmental evaluation revealed that Katy indeed had a mild form of attention deficit without hyperactivity. The psychological assessment showed that Katy was a happy child who generally felt good about herself and her world and had apparently suffered no loss of self-esteem. The testing was completed in June, and I recommended medication therapy to begin shortly before the start of school in September.

You might be interested in seeing copies of the "Work Habit" and "Conduct" sections of Katy's second and third grade report cards (pages 148 and 149)—exciting Before and After pictures illustrating the benefits of an appropriate diagnosis and remediation process.

Katy has done very well with combined medical and educational therapy. She takes methylphenidate twice daily and receives resource help at school to iron out specific problems and to assist her in improving her organizational skills. (Katy's teachers suggested this added assistance, and since the child did not qualify as learning disabled, I was able to recommend her for a special education program under the category of "Other Health Impaired.")

Therapy has done wonders for Katy's academic performance and for her overall outlook regarding school. She is now in the fourth grade and is making her highest grades ever.

This case study offers an excellent example of positive teacher intervention. Katy, having a mild case of attention deficit and being an intelligent child, was not an easy one to spot. It took a sensitive and loving teacher who cared enough to ask questions and find answers.

I would like to point out here that, since Katy's problems were truly attentional and were not primarily based upon her lack of maturity, it is most fortunate that she was not retained in any of the early grades. When a student has attention deficit that remains undiagnosed and untreated, that child will naturally continue to be distractible and maybe even immature despite her age or grade. Retention probably would not have accomplished anything in Katy's case and would be equally ineffective with many students with attention deficit.

Identifying the Older, Undiagnosed Students with Attention Deficit

Teachers of grades four through twelve should also be on the lookout for previously undiagnosed students with attention problems. There aren't as many of these children compared to those who are diagnosed in the earlier grades, but it is imperative that

2ND GRADE

Homeroom Teacher's Name _____ Jones _____ 19 85 19 86

	Reporting Period					
	1	2	3	4	5	6
Work Habits	N	N	N	N	N	N
Listens effectively	X	X	X	X	X	X
Follows directions	X	X	X	X	X	X
Makes good use of time	X	X	X	X	X	X
Contributes to group activities	✓	✓	✓	✓	✓	✓
Conduct	S-	N	S-	S	S	S+
Accepts responsibility for behavior	✓	X	✓	✓	✓	✓
Follows suggestions for improvement	X	X	X	✓	✓	✓
Observes classroom and school guidelines	X	X	X	X	X	✓
Cooperates with peers	✓	✓	✓	✓	✓	✓
Takes care of property	X	X	X	X	X	X

KEY: X, N — Needs improvement
  ✓, S — Satisfactory

they be recognized and helped. These are the students we talked about in Chapter Six who are usually of above-average intelligence and are able to get by in the earlier years by paying attention twenty to thirty percent of the time.

In the fourth and fifth grades, these students are suddenly required to perform more independently, creatively, and analytically. There is an added demand for personal expression, both oral and written, and organizational skills become essential.

Some of the students who display attention problems at this time, or even in junior high or high school, may have specific learning disabilities that they have been able to overcome or that were previously not as significant due to the style of learning used in the earlier studies. Others display no learning disorders or

3RD GRADE

Homeroom Teacher's Name ____Smith____ 19__86__ 19__87__

Reporting Period

	1	2	3	4	5	6
Work Habits	S	S+	S+	S+	S+	S+
Listens effectively	✓	✓	✓	✓	✓	✓
Follows directions	✓	✓	✓	✓	✓	✓
Makes good use of time	✓	✓	✓	✓	✓	✓
Contributes to group activities	✓	✓	✓	✓	✓	✓
Conduct	S	S+	S+	S+	S+	S+
Accepts responsibility for behavior	✓	✓	✓	✓	✓	✓
Follows suggestions for improvement	✓	✓	✓	✓	✓	✓
Observes classroom and school guidelines	✓	✓	✓	✓	✓	✓
Cooperates with peers	✓	✓	✓	✓	✓	✓
Takes care of property	✓	✓	✓	✓	✓	✓

KEY: X, N — Needs improvement
✓, S — Satisfactory

neurodevelopmental delays; they simply reach the point at which paying attention and concentrating on school work only part of the time will no longer make the grade.

So how can teachers recognize these older students with attention deficit? Naturally, these children will display some of the characteristics of the younger children, such as short attention span compared with other students their age, distractibility, free flight of ideas, impulsivity, mood swings, and social immaturity.

As I said earlier, these late elementary and secondary school students with attention deficit are frequently of above-average intelligence. Some of them come from high achieving homes where they have received much parental support and guidance. They probably made fairly high grades earlier in school but have shown a drastic decline as the demands of the educational system have increased.

At this point, in addition to all of the characteristics mentioned above, these students experience a great deal of frustration and are likely to display any or all of the following behaviors: acting out, not doing classwork, failing to turn in homework, and even cutting class. They may start to hang out with the wrong crowd, and they may turn to alcohol or drugs.

This type of conduct can indicate many very different types of problems. The teacher must carefully consider all the options, based on the child's past academic and behavioral history and on the child's current emotional state.

The student should be referred to the school counselor for help, by all means. The determination of the reason for the student's difficulties and the decision as to whether or not the child should be tested for learning or attention problems should be a conclusion arrived at by parents, teacher, counselor, and physician, working together for the benefit of the student.

Helping These Students in the Classroom

Once teachers know who the students with attention deficit are, and once these students are receiving appropriate medical therapy, if needed, there are many ways to help these individuals succeed in class. I would like to begin by offering some very general suggestions regarding classroom management of these students. I will then give some more specific guidelines for teachers at the different age levels—preschool, early elementary school, and late elementary and secondary school.

First of all, it is essential for the teacher to understand the entire child, rather than just looking at the attention deficit problem. In adopting any educational program for children with attention deficit, one must remember that this is a problem that, as we have seen, is sometimes associated with other learning difficulties. Unfortunately, the combination of two or three of these characteristics often takes on a cumulative effect, making their remediation much more complex and challenging. If a child with attention deficit also has a learning disability in the area of visual perception, for example, he will have a much greater problem than simply a child with either characteristic alone.

All students need love, understanding, and positive recognition. Perhaps these needs are even more important for students who have experienced frustration or failure, academically and/or socially. Students who have attention deficit need to know that there is someone who understands why they have trouble listening, reading, writing, or sitting still for a long time, and that they are not "dumb." They desperately need a teacher who cares enough to give them some positive attention and patient assistance.

Sometimes, in order to nurture the child with attention deficit and enhance her self-esteem, it becomes necessary for the teacher to evaluate the child's capabilities and set realistic goals for that student. For example, if the child simply cannot spell, it will do no good for her to take and fail a twenty-word spelling test each week. Perhaps the child could receive a grade for spelling the words orally, for copying each word five times, for making a crossword puzzle, for identifying a *correct* spelling when two choices are offered in print, or for matching words with definitions. Some children with attention deficit disorder have a great deal of trouble getting their thoughts on paper and may benefit from oral testing. For many of these pupils who have trouble completing assignments, the helpful modification could be as simple as shortening the amount of work required, so these kids can experience some satisfaction and success.

My final general suggestion for instructors at all levels regards discipline. Children with attention deficit will need to be disciplined—probably more often than other students will. A positive but firm approach, as we saw in Chapter Eight, is almost always the most beneficial.

Teachers may want to combine some of the following techniques: gently directing the child toward a more acceptable behavior—a distraction like a question or assignment of a chore may take his mind off the trip to Disneyworld or the idea of pulling Sara's ponytail; giving appropriate rewards for sincere attempts to improve conduct; and using behavior management techniques such as time-outs, contracts, and token economies, when needed. Embarrassing a student in front of his friends can be devastating to the child's self-concept and will probably only serve to increase or perpetuate misconduct. Talking to a child confidentially, whether in the hall or in an isolated area of the classroom, will have much better results. It is essential to address the particular action that was in violation of a rule without criticizing the child as a whole. The words "bad girl" and "bad boy" should be stricken from adults' vocabularies.

WHAT DO YOU DO WITH
A HYPERACTIVE CHILD IN PRESCHOOL?

Remember that the children who display obvious attention problems at ages two, three, or four are almost always hyperactive and sometimes have an associated conduct disorder; these children get into, out of, and on top of everything. They grab at whatever they can touch and sometimes get hold of items that adults think are safely out of reach. Teachers need to try to watch these children every minute.

The preschool teacher, therefore, must do his or her best to carefully observe children who have attention deficit and to constantly reinforce safe actions on the child's part. For example, comments such as, "I really liked the way you walked way around Eric's swing to get to yours," or "Thank you for asking me to help you get that book you couldn't reach," will serve to reinforce safe conduct.

Patience is probably the most valuable attribute of the pre-school teacher. This virtue is necessary in dealing with all very young children, but the hyperactive child will undoubtedly require an extra dose. Because these children are so active, impulsive, and distractible, they are, quite frankly, extremely frustrating to handle. They can be very moody and prone to violent tantrums, and the teacher must be able to handle this behavior with calm understanding.

As far as discipline is concerned, the time-out procedure probably works best with this age group. Since hyperactive children want to be constantly on the go, the idea of being required to sit down in a "Think It Over" chair for a few minutes is intensely distasteful. These children may throw an all-out screaming fit when asked to sit in time-out, but the experience will be so unpleasant that they will not want to have to do that again. If they bite, hit, throw a toy at, or push another child down shortly after time-out, the teacher should calmly enforce another time-out.

The time may come, on a particularly bad day, when the teacher may need to let the disruptive child go for a short visit to a time-out chair located in the preschool director's office. This total removal from the room may make a significant enough impact that the child will refrain from repeating that behavior.

Communication with the child's parents is essential. The parents need to know what is happening at school and what you, the teacher, are doing about it. In most cases, parents will be receptive to your information and concerns regarding their child. It is highly unlikely that anything you tell them will come as a surprise. Children are frequently on much better behavior at school than they are at home. Undoubtedly, the child's parents could tell you stories that would curl your hair!

If this child is consistently dangerous to himself and others or is so difficult to handle that he is wreaking havoc in the classroom, then something obviously must be done, and you, as the teacher, may be the only one at this point who has any grip on what the child's problem may be.

If you suspect an attention problem, then you should suggest that the parents go to the child's physician for guidance. If the parents tell you that they have already talked to the doctor and have been told that their child is just "all boy" or is "going through a stage," then be ready to recommend the name of a doctor who is knowledgeable about attention deficit and who can thoroughly evaluate the child and offer a second opinion.

Fortunately, many hyperactive children will be less difficult to control than those I've just described and will have patient and understanding parents who will be able to cope with the situation until the child reaches school age and really needs medical therapy. Behavioral and educational management are preferable to pharmacological treatment for preschoolers if possible.

The important thing to convey to the parents is your commitment as a teacher to providing a safe and happy learning experience for their child. When they realize your sympathy and concern, they will become staunch supporters of all your efforts.

TEACHING THE EARLY ELEMENTARY STUDENT WITH ATTENTION DEFICIT

Those hyperactive children who were able to survive preschool and home life without medication may be in a different boat once they start elementary school. Kindergarten tends to be much more structured than preschool, with greater sustained attention required from the students. Story times are longer, paperwork at the table is much more involved than at preschool, and there are many more rules and facts to be remembered. This can all be quite overwhelming for any kindergartner, and the hyperactive child may lose a lot of control. Some type of therapy may become necessary at this point. Following proper assessment and diagnosis, the physician, parents, psychologist, and teacher should collaborate to develop the optimal remediation process for that particular child.

Children with attention deficit who are not hyperactive usually have a milder reaction to the new demands placed upon them in elementary school. At some point, however, a sensitive teacher will pick up on these children's distractibility, short attention span, impulsivity, lack of organization, and inability to complete assignments.

There are many ways in which teachers can help these children to concentrate. A number of these methods will benefit the older children with attention deficit as well. However, I will present some more specific techniques aimed at those older students later in this chapter.

Providing Structure and Limiting Distractions

Most children with attention deficit seem to function best in structured situations. They don't always adjust well to changes in routine, and they really need understanding teachers who will make an effort to provide some consistency in environment and scheduling. If the teacher plans to be away from school for a few days, the children should be prepared to have a substitute. Whenever school situations or schedules are going to be altered, children with attention deficit will benefit from advance notice. These children find it easier to adjust to changes that they have anticipated.

Naturally, a child with attention difficulties needs to be in a structured classroom setting with minimal distractions. An open classroom or an area in which two or three activities are going on at one time is very disruptive for this type of individual.

Preferential seating of the child close to the instructor is also essential. In addition to minimizing distractions from other students, this enables the teacher to influence the child without disturbing the rest of the class.

At times, isolation of some sort may be extremely helpful for the student with attention deficit. A study carrel (even a makeshift folding cardboard screen) can minimize distractions. A large folding screen can be used to designate a special study area in a quiet corner. The child can even be sent to the library when she is having a particularly difficult time working in the classroom.

Please note that I am recommending only occasional isolation.

The child who has attention difficulties can also benefit tremendously from close proximity to the teacher and to students who are good role models. If she has trouble remembering what she is supposed to be doing, she can follow another student's example and catch up without asking the teacher a lot of questions.

Constant isolation can be damaging to the child's self-concept. Because she has attention deficit and is experiencing some difficulty in school, this child already feels different from, and perhaps inferior to, the other students. If she is required to work alone while other children are working in groups, she is likely to conclude that it is because she isn't as good or as smart as the others.

The mother of one of my patients told me about observing her daughter's kindergarten language arts class. (This was prior to the child's diagnosis with attention deficit.) The children sat in groups at tables, except for little Jessica, who was required to sit all by herself because she was talkative and easily distracted. The teacher gave directions for six different short assignments at the beginning of the fifty-minute class period, and the children were expected to complete one assignment, move to the next table and do the work laid out there, and so on. Jessica, because she was not in a group, was expected to remember all six sets of instructions and to complete them in order.

This expectation would have been too lofty for any five-year-old child working alone—not to mention one with the added difficulty of attention deficit. Most of the children working in groups managed to get by with the help of their friends. Jessica, studying alone, was lost.

Keeping the Child's Attention

The teacher and student may need to agree upon certain cues that will serve as reminders and bring the daydreaming or fidgeting child back to task. The teacher could gently touch the student's shoulder or tap his pencil on her desk to get her back on track. This technique may also be helpful when the child is displaying some mannerism or behavior that others may find annoying, such as biting nails, picking teeth, or drumming with a pencil. By giving the child a cue, the teacher hopefully will regain her attention and prevent her being teased by the other students.

Use of a timer on the child's desk may also prove effective. The teacher may want to offer a sticker or some special incentive for good work completed before the timer goes off. A reinforcement technique that has worked with many children is for the teacher to make a simple sticker book from construction paper. The child gets a sticker for each assignment completed within a designated time frame and places the sticker in his book. When the book is full, it may be redeemed for a special gift or privilege.

Giving Students a Break

Since prolonged concentration can be so tiring and frustrating for students with attention deficit, these children will need several breaks throughout the day so they can release tension and anxiety. A young class will benefit as a whole from regularly paced stretching exercises and relaxation techniques. The child with attention difficulties, especially, will need some authorized movement, whether it involves taking the attendance report to the office, watering the plants, or returning a book to the library.

In addition to providing rest and relaxation opportunities, these interludes will go a long way toward building the child's self-esteem. If the teacher gives the student some praise, affection, and recognition for carrying out such activities, the child will realize that he is an important part of the class, and he may begin to feel better about his abilities in general.

Helping Children Listen

There are many ways in which teachers can make it easier for their students to listen and pay attention. A number of these involve speaking and teaching skills on the part of the instructor.

First of all, it is imperative that the teacher speak clearly, loudly, and slowly enough. If children have trouble hearing or understanding what is being said, they will be easily distracted. Likewise, the teacher who talks faster than the students can listen will quickly lose their attention.

The teacher should also attempt to be aware of any personal

mannerisms or gestures that he or she has and that the children might find distracting. Children can get easily hung up on what a teacher is doing and totally miss what the teacher is saying.

In addition, we all know that a teacher's own enthusiasm for subject matter can heighten the students' interest. It is not easy for a teacher to present material in an interesting, enthusiastic manner hour by hour and day by day, but every attempt should be made to do so.

Humor goes hand in hand with enthusiasm and is an essential ingredient in good teaching. Most individuals, whether or not they have attention problems, enjoy jokes and comical anecdotes. Funny teachers tend to hold their students' attention and embellish facts with amusing touches that cling to memory.

Throughout oral presentations and readings, it is also important for the teacher to ask a lot of questions. An aptly timed question may bring a "wandering" student back to the fold, and involve that student in discussion. In fact, prior to giving a lecture or showing a film, the teacher might want to list some specific questions or ideas on the bulletin board so that students will attempt to listen for certain items. This will also positively reinforce key concepts and facts.

Of course, all of these suggestions regarding the cultivation of good listening skills will be beneficial to every student, not just to the child with attention deficit. But we can clearly see the importance of these techniques in teaching the child who can't concentrate.

Disciplining When Necessary

Again, I must advocate a positive approach to discipline. School and classroom rules should be defined clearly and should be understood by all students. Children with attention deficit, particularly the hyperactive ones, may break rules more often than other students. Their impulsivity, distractibility, social immaturity, and mood swings—which are all characteristic of ADD—can get these children into endless mischief. When children behave inappropriately, they need to be immediately and firmly disciplined.

With the early elementary school students, several types of positive discipline may be used. Time-out is probably the most effective disciplinary measure and can be carried out as described in Chapter Eight. For fairly minor offenses, creative techniques may be used, like removing the child's apple, pumpkin, snowman, or Easter bunny from the collection on the bulletin board. For using good manners, a quiet voice, kind words, etc., later in the day, the child may be allowed to restore his apple to its proper place on the class tree.

Another type of discipline, which involves communication with the parents, may be necessary for chronic offenders. The teacher may choose to send home "happy notes," tickets, or stickers to indicate that the child has had a good day at school. The parents may reward the child in some manner for a certain number of good reports.

The teacher may elect to enter into a behavioral contract with the child in an effort to eliminate inappropriate conduct. By using a chart, sticker book, checklist, or some other form of record keeping, the teacher will reward the child for his attempts to follow rules and to exhibit self-control. When the child fulfills the contract requirements, he will receive some predetermined award.

TEACHING THE OLDER
STUDENTS WITH ATTENTION DEFICIT

Many of the suggestions given above for minimizing distractions and fostering good listening skills are certainly applicable when dealing with the students who first experience attention problems in fourth or fifth grade or even much later. These children, who may have done fairly well in school prior to this time, may suddenly give indications of attention problems.

When these older students begin to experience academic or behavioral difficulties, they will need a lot of understanding. It would be easy for a teacher to become very frustrated with this type of individual who is clearly not working according to her potential. Nagging from teachers and parents will only serve to depress and confuse the child more, and the end result could be disastrous.

The best way to help one of these students is to begin with a sympathetic consultation with the child herself, offering sincere concern and a desire to get to the root of the child's problems. When students and teachers working cooperatively cannot solve a problem, it becomes time for parents, the counselor, and possibly a physician to become involved.

Frequently, discipline is necessary for these older students with attention deficit, and it may be that procedures like classroom token economies or contracts will prove most beneficial. A form of school grounding in which the disruptive young person is denied certain privileges, such as going to a pep rally, may work wonders.

The most important thing that teachers can offer to these older students is love. Students with attention deficit at this age are experiencing many physical and emotional changes, and they need your support.

Communication with Parents

Frequent communication with the home is absolutely essential. Teachers need to know if something stressful in the family situation has a potential for affecting the child's behavior or academic performance. Instructors may also need to coordinate other efforts with parents, such as making sure that homework assignments are copied correctly, necessary books are taken home, and assignments are completed and turned in. For students with attention deficit, these can be monumental tasks requiring a great deal of teacher/parent cooperation.

Overcoming Burn-Out

Helping children who have attention deficit to learn, achieve, and grow can be a most satisfying and rewarding experience, but it can also take its toll. At times, even those teachers with the best intentions can become frustrated with the consistent and disproportionate challenges and demands that these children can make. Teachers may need breaks or other types of assistance so they can become reenergized for the next challenge.

Sometimes, just talking about problems in the teacher's lounge can be helpful. Other teachers will have experienced similar difficulties and may be able to offer advice or humor.

Parents can also offer aid to the frustrated teacher, since they know better than anyone else what the teacher is going through. Teachers should turn to parents for support and for suggestions as to motivational techniques that tend to work with their children. Instructors should also make use of parent volunteers willing to perform certain classroom jobs such as mimeographing, cutting, and decorating bulletin boards, freeing the teacher to do other things.

Parent support groups welcome educational personnel, and their meetings and programs can be very informative for classroom teachers. Parents tend to ask speakers a lot of questions about classroom handling of children who have attention deficit, and teachers will pick up a lot of pointers in these sessions.

Most importantly, perhaps, teachers need to get away from the profession for a night or a weekend. The world won't end if the spelling papers don't get graded—teaching does not always have to be a twelve-hour-a-day, seven-day-a-week job. Breaks and mini-vacations from teaching can bring needed revitalization and refreshment, enabling the teacher to continue to impart knowledge to students of all kinds.

11.

Attention Deficit Problems in Adults

Considering all the medical and lay coverage that has been given to the problems associated with attention deficit during the past five years, one would think that the word would be out that ADD does not miraculously disappear during adolescence, as previously thought. However, it is apparently not yet public knowledge that attention difficulties continue into adulthood. The belief that attention deficit is outgrown is still so pervasive that it is often difficult to convince parents that their children (who may have been doing great on treatment) really need to continue that treatment at least through the turbulent years of early adolescence.

Why Adults Still Have Attention Deficit

The idea of patients somehow miraculously outgrowing this problem really has no scientific basis. Indeed, I am not convinced that any individuals with attention deficit ever totally outgrow their difficulty. What I have witnessed is that children who are successfully supported either behaviorally, medically, educationally, or, most often, using all three treatment methods, learn to recognize and adjust to their symptoms. They can do quite well in most circumstances without the assistance of medication once they reach a certain level of maturity (which most frequently comes when they are in high school). Another reason for the myth that this syndrome is outgrown is related to the fact that certainly hyperactive individuals do display less overt activity as they mature. Unfortunately, however, many of the other characteristics persist and often lead to increasing difficulties in adulthood, especially if they are not effectively treated in childhood.

Just as in all discussions thus far, we do need to add a small qualifier. As we saw in Chapter Six, there are some individuals with attention deficit who are not diagnosed until they reach junior high school, when the demands of the educational system require different skills. On the other hand, there are also some individuals with mild forms of attention deficit with some specific learning disabilities that may affect them in early elementary school but become less significant in middle childhood. Because of this, as these individuals approach junior high school, they can gain more control over their impulsivity and distractibility and thus no longer need the assistance of any pharmacological therapy.

What we are seeing is not the fact that these students have outgrown their attention problems, but, instead, that they have learned to compensate for their learning difficulty so that it is no longer a major disability for them. Without a specific learning problem accompanying the milder forms of attention deficit, these students can control their selective attention and organizational difficulties well enough on their own that many of their symptoms certainly seem to be less notable than they were in the early childhood years. I have seen this several times. Some children who initially benefit from medication may no longer need it as they approach high school. Unfortunately, this is the minority of the individuals with whom I come in contact.

If we look back to the physiological model, this all makes sense. There is no reason why we should suddenly see a more efficient production or usage of neurotransmitters that would make attention deficit suddenly disappear in adolescence or adulthood. An interesting observation that has become readily apparent to me after working with these children for several years is the familial nature of this problem. Many children with attention deficit have a parent who had learning problems as a child and who still has trouble concentrating at times, even though he or she may have learned to cope with the lack of focus and may function acceptably in the adult world. Attention deficit in adults is now recognized by the medical community and is referred to as ADD-Residual Type (ADD-RT).

Characteristics of Attention Deficit Residual Type

In looking at the characteristics of attention deficit in adults, we find that there are many similarities to the childhood manifestations; however, there are some unique characteristics as well. One of the similarities to childhood attention deficit is that most adults are really unaware of the symptoms, since they have been dealing with these difficulties their entire life. Although unaware, they are very frustrated by their problems and feel helpless to change them in any meaningful or permanent way.

Adult symptoms frequently appear in a more subtle manner than those of children. Since physicians do not see overt hyperactivity per se in adults (as we do not see it in two thirds of the children as well), we rely on other characteristics for diagnosis. Unfortunately, since adults with attention deficit are no longer enclosed in a controlled environment where their behaviors are closely monitored (such as in a classroom), it becomes increasingly difficult to pick out these symptoms. However, in looking at the characteristics, the similarities to childhood attention deficit are striking.

INABILITY TO FOCUS

Adults with attention deficit continue to have problems with selective attention that make it difficult for them to concentrate for any period of time on tasks they do not enjoy. Like their childhood counterparts, they do much better focusing on material that they find very interesting than on other material that is not as interesting but may be very important to their jobs or families. They tend to be distracted by any disturbances in the environment around them.

Many adults who have attention difficulties will complain that they are unable to keep their minds on conversations and are continually aware of other stimuli (no matter how minor) in their surrounding environment. They dislike parties where they are encompassed by multiple conversations. They find it hard to play bridge when there is more than one table, because they sometimes hear talk from another table and lose track of the bidding or the playing of the cards. They have trouble concentrating on lectures or sermons and may even be unable to sit through lengthy television shows or movies. These individuals may have great difficulty sustaining attention for reading or for written work, particularly if the subject matter is lacking in excitement.

When adults with attention deficit do concentrate, they may have to do it so intently that they effectively block out contact to the outside world and will not immediately hear someone calling them. The adult with attention deficit who is engrossed in a television show, book, newspaper, or work on a computer may truly not hear things that are said to him or calls to the dinner table. One spouse of an individual with attention deficit related that she resorted to calling, "Fire!" to get her husband's attention. This method does work, but may not foster family harmony. Another wife told me that she literally has to shake her spouse to get his attention when he is watching a sporting event. The husband who has attention deficit is not consciously ignoring his wife; he just invests so much energy in sustaining his attention that the rest of the world is blocked out. Unfortunately, this individual may be misunderstood by others as being rude or unsociable in situations where he or she is being bombarded with stimuli and is simply trying to concentrate on one thing.

POOR ORGANIZATION

Organizational skills are also problematic for adults with attention deficit. As students, these individuals rarely brought the right book home and almost never turned in their homework assignments, even if they managed to finish them the night before. As adults, they frequently forget appointments, are perpetually late, and have great difficulty in organizing anything ahead of time, such as trips, parties, or even dinner. An activity such as cleaning the home may result in half the wash being completed, one of the two bathrooms getting cleaned, and dinner being only half-cooked, with several starts but multiple distractions that prevent completion.

Distractibility results in the shifting from one task to the next. It can be brought on by a very slight deviation. For example, if an adult who has attention deficit is mowing the lawn, and the bag that catches the grass becomes filled, this individual may make a trip to the garage to empty the bag. He may then note that the car needs to be moved, which may result in his realizing that the oil in the car needs to be changed. The result is that the mowing job gets put on hold.

MOOD SHIFTS

Mood swings seem to be more pronounced in adulthood than in childhood. Many individuals with ADD-RT relate shifting from a normal mood to a mild depression that can last for hours to several days. This can then switch to a mild euphoria that also can last for hours or even a few days.

Again, we are talking about a degree. Their emotional instability is not like that of an individual with a bipolar mental illness who will alternate between a major psychotic depression where she cannot deal with work and a manic phase where she is on a nonstop high. Individuals with attention deficit tend to experience mood shifts that are more subtle, but definitely identifiable. They will describe periods where they are down and nearly at a loss to do anything about it and then periods of feeling good, sociable, more productive at work, and more positive about their relationships. It should be noted that these mood shifts can occur spontaneously, but are more often related to specific triggering episodes. Such an episode may be a seemingly insignificant occurrence, which, on another day or under different circumstances, might elicit a very different response from the same individual. However, on that particular day, the episode can have a completely mood-altering effect.

IMPULSIVITY

Individuals who have attention deficit/residual type are also characterized by impulsive decisions with poor tolerance of stress. Most of these adults will experience some problems that are directly related to their impulsivity. They may have financial difficulties due to impulsive buying habits and risky investments, trouble on the job because of hasty decision making, and social problems brought on by impulsive words and actions.

In the more severely involved adults, their behaviors often result in frequent job changes or moves, multiple marriages or affairs, and drug or alcohol abuse. As with their childhood counterparts, routines are often important to adults with attention deficit. When these routines are disrupted (which is often the case due to the poor organization and impulsivity of these adults), the individuals become very stressed, often experiencing depression and anger.

Occasionally, a subgroup of these individuals (and again, probably those with more severe cases of attention deficit) may display hot-tempered, explosive outbursts that may even be frightening to these people, who feel overwhelmed and powerless to do anything about their outbursts. At times, this impulsivity can even lead to some violent acts with severe repercussions and may interfere with many ongoing personal relationships. This unfortunately often results in multiple crises in dealing with many of the routine life stresses. This can also lead these individuals to a feeling of general dissatisfaction with their lives, which is tragic, since many of them, as we have seen, are bright, capable people.

In a milder form, attention deficit/residual type will result in mood alterations, temper outbursts, and constant activity with a very difficult time relaxing. The difference in the degree of impulsivity is probably related not only to the severity of the attention impairment but also to the support and treatment these individuals received as children and young adults. Frustration and lack of self-esteem will certainly serve to perpetuate any symptoms already present.

SOCIAL PROBLEMS

Some individuals with attention deficit will overcome their social immaturity as they grow older. They will learn social skills and will gain confidence in situations that require those skills. These people will finally be able to maintain friendships.

Others with attention deficit will continue to have social difficulties in adulthood for various reasons. They may alienate acquaintances because of their impulsivity and mood swings. They may tend to be aggressive or domineering in an attempt to get ahead (or catch up). They may interrupt other people when a thought comes to them, because they are afraid they'll forget what they wanted to say. They may even appear to ignore others when they are locked into concentrating on something important at the time.

For whatever reasons, many adults who have the residual type of attention deficit experience social difficulties of varying sorts and find themselves short on friends. The mother of a fourteen-year-old with attention difficulties recently told me that she could understand her son's social problems. She said that she had experienced the same difficulties as a child and even as a younger adult. She had only been successful in keeping friends for about the past ten years.

Adults with attention deficit may really need to work at friendships. By trying to overcome self-centeredness, moodiness, and impulsivity in their relationships with others, they may be able to improve their socialization skills and hold on to friends.

Making a Diagnosis

It must be remembered that, when dealing with these adults, just as in dealing with children who have attention deficit, many of the associate characteristics that they display can be related to other illnesses or difficulties. When these characteristics are taken out of context, one must rule out personality disorders or other psychiatric difficulties.

All of us as adults can look at one or two of these characteristics and state, "That fits," or "I can relate to that aspect of the disorder." It is important to remember, however, that fewer than ten percent of the population have attention deficit. As I said in Chapter Two, it is the severity of the symptoms and their combined detrimental effect on an individual's life that indicate that a person has attention deficit. One must look at the entire picture from childhood on and do appropriate diagnostic assessments geared to adults, to make the appropriate diagnosis.

Studies such as that performed by Klee et. al, published in *Psychiatric Annals* of November 1986, have shown that an objective measure such as the Continuous Performance Task (CPT) or the Wechsler Adult Intelligence Scale–Revised (WAIS-R) is helpful. Steven H. Klee, Ph.D., Barry D. Garfinkel, M.D., and Hortense Beauchesne, R.N., compared responses of twelve adult males who had been diagnosed and treated for attention deficit as children with a volunteer control group of twelve adult males matched for educational level with the index group. Participants selected for the control group had no documented history of attention deficit or psychiatric disorders. None of the subjects took stimulant medication at the time of testing.

The CPT, which was programmed in Pascal using an Apple II computer, consisted of ten different letters flashing randomly on a screen for 130 milliseconds, with 500 milliseconds between letters. The task was to press a bar when the letter *S* appeared followed by the letter *T*, and to avoid responding to other letter groupings. All test participants were exposed to 500 letters, ten percent of which were targets. An error of omission was scored every time a target was missed, and errors of commission were recorded when the subjects responded to non-target stimuli. A composite score of the total number of omissions and commissions was also determined.

Results of the testing were very interesting. The index group with attention deficit committed more omission errors and had a higher summary score of omissions and commissions than did the control group. This scoring seems to offer a clear indication that adults who have attention deficit tend to act more impulsively than do adults who do not have the problem.

The coding and arithmetic subtests of the Wechsler Adult Intelligence Scale–Revised were also administered. These WAIS-R subtests had been previously shown to correlate with continuous task performance, in that responses were influenced to a degree by attention span and distractibility. Raw scores on the two subtests were converted into scaled scores for statistical comparison, and interesting results were obtained.

The index group of adults with attention deficit responded similarly to the control group on the arithmetic subtest. It may be that the adult version of the arithmetic subtest is not sensitive enough to measure group differences. Perhaps most people, by adulthood, have mastered the skills involved in this test (matching, arithmetic calculation, and scanning). This may explain the similarity in scores between the two adult groups.

Results of the Digit Symbol (or coding) subtest were a different story. The index group scored significantly lower than the control group. Poor performance on the Digit Symbol subtest, in studies with children, has been found to correspond with difficulties in new learning situations, as well as in concentration and tracking. Therefore, the index group, identified as having attention deficit in childhood, clearly displayed continuing attention difficulties when compared with adults who did not have attention deficit.

The index group also differed significantly from the control group in self-rating of childhood behaviors. Both groups were asked to fill out modified versions of the Conners' Teacher Rating Scale, a scale used to help identify students with attention deficit. The subjects were given a 47-item checklist regarding childhood characteristics, as well as a 42-item questionnaire assessing current behavioral characteristics. The checklists assessed motor activity, selective attention difficulties, organization, peer relations, mood, temper, and medical problems. The index group reported more childhood behavioral difficulties than the control group and saw themselves as having been more active, restless, impulsive, and nervous than the other adults tested. The index group also remembered more concentration problems and poorer frustration tolerance during childhood. Such behavior differences were not indicated in the comparison of current behaviors, because the index group reported themselves as much improved.

All adults with attention deficit had their problems as children, with the symptoms persisting into adulthood, rather than developing in adulthood. Indeed, many psychiatrists speak of this as a distinguishing characteristic of ADD, since individuals who have developed specific psychiatric illnesses can recognize a change in the way they feel or relate, but untreated individuals with attention deficit have lived with the problem throughout their lives and thus will not be aware of any change in their feelings or reactions.

One of the interesting parts of talking to adults with this problem is that, despite their increasing sophistication, they still do not recognize the source of their feelings in relationship to the attention problem. An example of this is a recent article in the *The New York Times Magazine* of October 11, 1987, where a young author named Frank Wolkenberg describes the agony he went through for years until he was correctly diagnosed at the age of thirty and appropriately treated. He vividly describes his feelings of isolation and repeated frustration that drove him to the brink of suicide. The relief of being able to identify the reason for his difficulty, accompanied by the sense of total frustration of having lived with the problem while being unaware of its global effect on his life, was indeed overwhelming for him. This and many stories quite similar are becoming increasingly common to those of us who care for children and adults with this problem.

In dealing with children and spending time describing attention deficit characteristics in detail to unsuspecting parents, I often encounter a parent who has the sudden realization that she is listening to a modified synopsis of her own development. In fact, these parents are probably the lucky ones, since many of the more seriously affected adults are unable to stick with an ongoing relationship long enough to even be present at their children's evaluation for this problem. Again, we must emphasize, as we did throughout our childhood descriptions, that there is a strong need for a careful and controlled diagnosis by an individual or team that is experienced in diagnosing and treating these patients.

DALE

I would like to present a case study of an individual with ADD-RT, even though I deal in pediatric medicine and do not diagnose or treat adults myself. Dale is one of those parents who, when listening to my discussion of attention deficit upon the diagnosis of his child, recognized that I was retelling the story of his own life and his own academic and social difficulties.

Dale never did well in school as a child. He hated most of his teachers and was certain that most of them disliked him as well. Dale never could get all of his work done. His teachers thought he was lazy, and everyone thought he should be able to make better grades. He just couldn't listen in class or read assignments without daydreaming. Even when he wanted to read or to hear something, his mind seemed to wander. He was never really with the rest of the class.

Getting assignments completed and turned in was always a problem for Dale. He never could spell and he had great difficulty when asked to copy anything from a blackboard. In his struggle to concentrate on copying large numbers of words that he could not spell, Dale inevitably left out letters and words and had trouble keeping his writing on the lines.

It was inconceivable to Dale how anyone could complete a vocabulary assignment. He remembers the frustration of being told to look up twenty words in the dictionary, copy the definitions, and write a story using all twenty words. Just finding the words in the dictionary and writing down the definitions in the allotted time was an incomprehensible task for him. Dale never even got as far as attempting to use the words in sentences.

Dale had to repeat the second and fifth grades. Since his father was in the Army and they moved frequently, he ended up in three different schools during his first year in second grade. He missed one-third of that school year while in transit between bases—so the retention was understandable. Fifth grade, however, was another story altogether. Dale had an immense dislike for his teacher and still remembers a class requirement that he found impossible. He was supposed to memorize the names of all forty-eight states and their capitals and had to be able to write and spell those names correctly. He just couldn't do it.

Junior high and high school were also hard, because Dale could not read a textbook without his mind wandering. He was never able to complete a reading assignment. He got to where he didn't even try. Dale was able to make passing grades due to his own knowledge of the subject matter or because of information occasionally picked up in class when he happened to be tuned in to the teacher. Dale managed to make Bs in science, math, and industrial arts, and to squeak by with Cs or Ds in English and social studies. Term papers terrified Dale. In fact, he never really wrote one. He simply copied enough information from books to produce D papers so he could pass.

Dale was never considered hyperactive. He just couldn't concentrate sufficiently. One of Dale's three brothers was diagnosed as hyperactive, however, and doctors considered the whole family to be accident-prone. The four boys were frequently turning up in Army medical center emergency rooms with broken or fractured bones, lacerations, burns, etc. The boys were all impulsive and fearless. They revelled in adventure—rarely stopping to look before leaping. The consequences were sometimes painful.

Socially, Dale frequently had problems as a child. He was pretty much of a loner. He cannot remember the names of any of the children that he knew in elementary school. Dale feels that he was an obnoxious child who alienated others due to his domineering behavior. He thinks that he always talked too much and annoyed others by dominating conversations. He always felt compelled to say something as soon as it flashed into his mind (even if it meant interrupting someone), because the thought might be lost a few moments later. Dale was in high school before he developed any close friends—and then only a few. But those individuals are still his friends—twenty-five years later.

After completing high school, Dale gave college a very short and predictably frustrating try, before joining the Army. Actually, the Army was an excellent place for Dale. Structure was imposed. Organization was assumed and was required. There was no option. Flight school had regular nightly study halls that were quiet, or else. . . . Dale responded well to the structure of the military.

Dale became a good helicopter pilot. The job was structured; everything he needed was close at hand. He flew Army ambulance copters in Vietnam and went home with a Distinguished Flying Cross for picking up wounded soldiers under intense enemy fire.

He returned to the States to become an instructor pilot back at the flight school, where he continued to do well under imposed organization. He was soon made a lieutenant, and, a year later, a captain.

Following marriage, Dale continued to thrive in his military career as the commander of a basic training company. It was only when that job ended and the desk jobs began that his attention difficulties started to resurface. Administrative desk jobs were necessary for advancement, and Dale was made Plans Officer, with the responsibility for writing post contingency plans, such as for ice removal. Some of these plans were supposed to be hundreds of pages long, and they were mind-boggling for Dale.

His next change of station brought another unlikely assignment—that of Post Information Officer. Dale became editor of the post newspaper. It was a good thing that he had married an English major. But since Dale was no longer experiencing personal success on the job, the Army lost its appeal. There were no more flying jobs to be had, and Dale breathed a sigh of relief when the Army found it necessary to reduce forces and lay him off in 1973 with several thousand other pilots whose services were no longer needed because of the end of the Vietnam War.

Much as he loved flying, Dale saw no practical career opportunity there, and he returned to school to pursue a degree in electronics engineering. It wasn't easy, but he had chosen a trade school that required a limited number of nontechnical courses. His interest in electronics aided in his concentration, and he found that he could even read things that did not interest him if he would point to each word with a pencil. In order to really concentrate, Dale had to effectively shut out everything that was going on around him. This required a great deal of effort. Dale would become so totally absorbed in his work (or in a science-fiction book or a television show) that it was difficult for anyone to get his attention away from that focus. Dale finally succeeded in earning his degree.

Dale performed reasonably well as an electronics engineer, although he experienced some problems with organization and concentration. He was often forgetful and found that his memory was inconsistent. He seemed to have a phenomenal long-term memory including vast numbers of details (some relevant and some not). He could tell, without fail, after reading two or three pages of a book, if he had ever read it before, and he would remember all of the details of the story. He never forgot anything about a movie, no matter how long it had been since he had seen it.

His short-term memory for important details regarding his job was less reliable, however. He would frequently misplace things and forget to do things that he was supposed to get done. His wife would remind him to get his lunch out of the refrigerator before leaving for work, and, two minutes later, he would go out the door without it.

But work went pretty well, and Dale remained happy in his home life with his wife and two young children. He did not hear of attention deficit until his first child was diagnosed at age seven. It was only then that he realized that he had been living with this difficulty for forty years and that it had probably been the cause of most of his difficulties in school.

Dale confided his own attention difficulties to me that day in my office, and I recommended that he talk to his family physician, since I was not comfortable treating adults. I gave Dale copies of forty pages worth of articles on ADD-RT for his doctor to read, and—after several weeks of study—that doctor agreed to treat Dale. The family physician prescribed 20 milligrams of methylphenidate (Sustained Release Ritalin) for Dale daily.

The results were immediate. Dale reported instantaneous improvement at work. He became much more organized and more productive. When reading or paperwork was required, Dale saw a tremendous improvement in his concentration and performance. There are still days that are less than perfect, but, overall, life looks rosier now. Dale feels much better about himself and his ability to succeed on the job, and that self-confidence carries over to his interactions with friends and family.

Treatment of Adults

Before an adult who has attention deficit can be helped, he or she must recognize that there is a problem. As I mentioned earlier, adults with attention deficit have lived with their characteristics for years and have learned to compensate for some of these problems. Even if they have not coped particularly successfully, most of these individuals think that they are normal. They may be very resistant to anyone's suggestion that they have a "disorder," and they may also object to the idea that their children have anything wrong with them. When diagnosing a child, I occasionally find that one of the parents will object to the diagnosis, saying, "There's nothing wrong with my kid. He's just like me." Unfortunately, that's exactly the problem, but it's hard to make a parent see it.

Of course, a lot of parents with undiagnosed attention deficit are like Dale. When I explain why their children are having trouble in school, they realize that this is something that they have experienced themselves. It is a tremendous relief for these people to realize that there was a reason for their academic and social difficulties.

A person who is willing to concede that he or she may have an attention problem can be evaluated and assisted with therapies similar to those that are used with children. In Chapter Twelve, "Finding Help," I will offer some suggestions regarding how an adult can find an appropriate doctor, and I will provide information regarding organizations that may be helpful for the adult with attention deficit.

Once the correct diagnosis is made, we are then again dealing with a physiological disorder that will respond well to medical as well as behavioral treatment and counseling. Since the basic physiology is not different from that of children with attention deficit, many of the same drugs are employed for adults.

Before discussing the medications used with adults, I would like to bring up the matter of caffeine. I have found in talking to parents with attention problems that many of these individuals, most often fathers, have been mildly treating themselves with caffeine for years. Although caffeine has a minimal stimulation effect in children with attention deficit, adults will often consume large quantities (six to twenty cups of coffee per day or perhaps a liter of Coca-Cola or Dr. Pepper) that seem to produce a mild stimulation of the neurotransmission process so that they can be more relaxed and focused at their jobs or at home. Interestingly enough, most of these adults are totally unaware of the increased ability to focus and complete their work until it is pointed out to them.

Just this week I evaluated a young man with hyperactivity accompanied by conduct disorder whose father had experienced tremendous difficulty in school (dropping out in the seventh grade). The father now has a job working where he is moving about continually, and he is always engaged in some activity around the home. When I asked his wife how much coffee he consumed a day, she stated, "Five or six pots" (20–30 cups). Since he has always done that, she did not consider it out of the ordinary. Indeed, this individual has been treating himself, at least partially, for all of his adult life, allowing himself to function both at work and at home, although still displaying many of the other symptoms. Caffeine does help, but only to a limited degree.

MEDICAL TREATMENT
The determination of which adults should be treated, for how long, and in what manner, must be individualized between the patient and the physician in charge of his care. Just as in children, every case is unique, and thus every treatment plan must be individualized as well. Keeping that in mind, let us look at the three types of medications that seem to be most beneficial for adults with attention deficit:

1. Stimulants.

Stimulants again form the first line of therapy. As noted in the case presentation, adults' responses to the medication are similar to those of children. Adults will experience increased ability to attend to work and social situations and decreased impulsivity and motor activity. Individuals with attention deficit/residual type often report more productivity and efficiency at work, less stress due to everyday common nuisances both at work and at home, and general feelings of increased personal satisfaction. They also note fewer mood fluctuations, and, even more importantly, fewer temper outbursts. I have had several spouses relate tremendous improvements in their marriages and family life following treatment of their respective mates.

Dr. Paul Wender and his colleagues, who have done a great deal of research on adult attention deficit at the University of Utah, published an article in *The American Journal of Psychiatry* in May 1985, where they looked at thirty-seven adult patients meeting the Utah criteria for ADD-RT. They found that twenty-one of them had a moderate-to-marked response to methylphenidate, while only four of the thirty-seven had a response to placebo. Again, the patients noted improved attention, decreased impulsivity, and decreased emotional fluctuations. Subjects generally were reported to be happier and more productive, with fewer mood swings. They experienced less anger, tension, and depression. Side effects of the medication seem to be similar (see Chapter Seven) to the effects found in treating children. Most of these side effects were short-lived.

Since amphetamine and methylphenidate are drugs that can be abused, many physicians and psychiatrists are reluctant to prescribe them for adults. Individuals with attention deficit/residual type are often very impulsive. Some may have had trouble with alcohol or drug abuse in the past. It is understandable why a doctor would hesitate to treat such an individual with a drug having the potential for abuse. But this is an unfortunate situation, since the stimulants are the drugs most likely to help these individuals.

2. Tricyclic antidepressants.

The tricyclics, such as imipramine and desipramine, are sometimes used, but these drugs have not appeared to be as effective with adults as in the special groups of children with whom I used these medications.

3. MAO Inhibitors.

These medications were formerly used as antidepressants in adults. Dr. Wender and his colleagues have looked at the MAO Inhibitors as being useful for some adults with attention deficit. These particular medications have potentially more serious side effects, including dangerous elevation of blood pressure when taken with certain foods or drugs, as well as a possible reduction in blood pressure when standing up suddenly. Safe use of the MAOIs requires avoidance of aged cheeses and red wines in particular, along with certain other foods and medications. The MAO Inhibitors are thus not as popular to use for ADD-RT.

As far as we know, and, again, the drugs mentioned above have been used and studied for several decades, with the appropriate diagnosis and ongoing management, they appear to be very safe and in many cases an extremely significant positive treatment method that can have tremendous favorable influences on the quality of life for these individuals as well as for their families.

PSYCHOLOGICAL AND BEHAVIORAL TREATMENT
Of course, as I have stressed repeatedly throughout this book, there is no cure for attention deficit. Medication can help greatly, but, for many patients it is not enough. Just as we saw in adolescents who have struggled with ADD for a long time and have begun to act out, many adults with these problems have been overwhelmed by their struggle and frustrations in dealing with their individual symptoms. Most, if treated medically, will probably benefit from some ongoing psychological counseling in conjunction with the medical therapy. Thirty years of frustration cannot be erased with one pill. It is essential to help these individ-

uals understand and recognize how much of their problem is physiological and how much is secondary to psychological manifestations from dealing with this problem for so many years.

Adults who have attention deficit need the support of their families and friends. It may help immeasurably for the patient's spouse, parent, or significant other to be involved in the treatment process—to talk with the physician or psychologist and learn everything possible about attention deficit. Since most adults who are diagnosed with ADD consider themselves normal, they may resist medication or counseling and may need the encouragement of those who are close to them.

Caring friends and family members may be able to help the adult with attention deficit in many ways. They may find ways of alerting this individual to an undesirable behavior before it becomes a major problem (just as the teacher or parent gives cues to the child who has attention difficulties). Humor can work wonders to avert a potentially awkward situation.

Significant others can also assist the adult with ADD-RT in bringing some order to his or her life. There are all kinds of "organizers" that can work wonders if used diligently—desk, drawer, and closet organizers, file cabinets, storage boxes. The adult with attention deficit will also benefit from using planning calendars, appointment books, expense and travel logs, etc. Lists of chores and goals will be of great value.

With the help of those around him and with appropriate treatment, this adult can experience a whole new appreciation of life. As Wolkenberg stated in his essay in *The New York Times Magazine*, "The first day after starting to take medication, walking down the Brooklyn street on which I then lived, I noticed the sky through the leaves of a tree and stopped to look at it. After a minute, it struck me that for the first time in my life, I was looking at something with no sensation of having to stop and move on."

12.

Finding Help

We have now reviewed our subject matter extensively. I have examined the various types of attention deficit in the different age groups and have discussed the many treatment options.

Perhaps now the most important bit of information is where you can go to obtain the appropriate assistance if you indeed feel that your child may have this difficulty. As I have tried to stress to you throughout the book, there can be many reasons for inattention. Certainly, not every child who has trouble concentrating in class has a primary attention deficit. Furthermore, as we have seen, not all children who do have primary attention deficit can be treated in the same manner. This, of course, leads us back to another common theme, upon which I have also focused: how can you protect yourself and your child from not only the old forms of fad therapies that have proliferated, but also from new ones that may appear tomorrow? There is much to consider as we embark upon a path to help children, and this task may involve a great deal of time and energy. However, it must be continually emphasized that, with the appropriate assessment and remediation, the result can be a well-adjusted and happy individual who, at the very least, has an opportunity to pursue a career and life of his or her choosing.

If, after reading this book, you do suspect that your child has attention deficit, you probably have very mixed feelings. You are relieved that there may be a medical explanation for your child's academic and behavioral problems, but you are concerned about where you should go from here. You read a best-selling book that states that all of your child's attention and learning problems can be solved by dietary changes. You hear on a talk show that the medication used to treat attention deficit has harmful side effects. Then you see a magazine ad claiming that six 20-minute, $500 sessions with a specialist will cure your child forever. You are bombarded by the media with conflicting information, and it is hard to know which expert to trust.

You have to do something. You love your child. You want to help him overcome his attention deficit so he can succeed academically and socially, and so he can feel good about himself. Above all, you want your child to be happy.

Where Is a Parent to Turn?

So, what do you do? I would suggest—no, plead—that you take your child to a physician or clinic that is experienced in treating attention difficulties.

I have emphasized to you and strongly believe that a physician needs to be a part of both the assessment and, of course, the treatment process. This is essential for two reasons. The first is that the student needs a multidisciplinary approach to this multi-dimensional problem. Although educational behavioral psychologists or social workers are an integral part of this team, they do not work with the medical aspects of this problem and certainly are not licensed to prescribe the appropriate medication when needed. Secondly, as we have seen, an important part of the physician's role is to continually serve as patient advocate, protecting patients from the inappropriate treatments that can abound in a community.

In my practice in California alone, approximately ten to fifteen percent of my patients have seen behavioral optometrists, spending anywhere from $2,000 to $4,000 for a remedy that is absolutely useless (at least in its relationship to attention deficit disorder).

Whether this type of therapy has any merit at all in treating dyslexia is a little bit less clear; however, as I pointed out in Chapter Seven, the evidence is sketchy at best. So we can thus see that the physician really plays a key role in the areas of treatment and patient advocacy.

I therefore recommend (as I have said earlier) that you turn to a physician or a team that includes a physician, but I must be more specific. Several types of professionals work with attention deficit patients. Possible evaluators include behavioral pediatricians, as well as child psychologists, pediatric neurologists, child psychiatrists, and others. There is obviously much crossover here; however, I do have my own particular bias.

First, I think that a pediatric neurologist, although excellent in taking care of neurological disabilities or severe neurological handicaps in children, usually does not have the time to devote to adequately caring for a child with an attention problem. In addition to the important diagnostic evaluations, the care of a child who has attention deficit involves ongoing follow-up for the modulation of medication and the supervision of educational issues. Children with attention deficit do not have what was formerly referred to as minimal brain damage. These children take time and need coordination in a team approach to diagnose and subsequently follow their progress. Most pediatric neurologists are simply too busy to take on patients with attention deficit. This, of course, is not to say that pediatric neurologists who are interested in attention deficit and are willing to devote their time in this area cannot do an excellent job. Certainly they can. I am merely saying that the vast majority of these doctors do not have time to treat attention deficit and are probably not the best individuals to care for these children.

Child psychiatrists have both the knowledge of the behavioral interactions of these children as well as the psychopharmacology needed to adequately deal with their problems. These professionals, if interested in treating attention deficit disorder, can be a valuable resource. Unfortunately (except in larger metropolitan areas), there is a shortage of trained child psychiatrists who can use this expertise. I do not believe that adult psychiatrists have the appropriate training and experience to evaluate children with attention deficit in most cases.

This, of course, leaves a behaviorally oriented pediatrician who is usually more available and recognizes the time commitment needed to assist these children adequately. These physicians usually see children from birth through adolescence and become extremely familiar with the different presentations of attention deficit as well as with the natural progression of this process. Even more importantly, they are able to deal with different members of the mental health and educational communities so that they can coordinate all the remediation efforts.

Finding the
Appropriate Doctor

Knowing how to locate such an individual is essential. Whether this person is a child psychiatrist, pediatric neurologist, or behavioral pediatrician, the most important part of the equation is finding an individual who is sensitive to your child's needs and will devote the time and resources needed to assist you. To find such a person, you must look throughout the community for various sources of information to try to get a sense of who is the most appropriate professional.

First, since school teachers and especially counselors deal with medical personnel regarding students with various learning problems, these educators will probably know which doctors can be trusted to perform reputable evaluations and treatments. Ask the school to provide names of professionals who have evaluated other students at that institution.

You should also ask your friends for suggestions. Attention deficit is not rare. Almost everyone knows someone who has been diagnosed with this problem. Parents of children with attention deficit may be an excellent source of information. Many will be quite willing to offer advice, since they once experienced anxiety like yours.

Numerous communities have support groups to help both

parents and children cope with this disorder. The Association for Children and Adults with Learning Disabilities (ACLD) has chapters in most metropolitan areas and can be an extremely valuable resource. Your ACLD group may be able to provide you with a list of recommended physicians. If their suggestions are not in writing, they will probably be happy to talk with you about the treatment that is available in the area. (You will find further information on ACLD later in this chapter.)

Being a Wise Consumer

After finally selecting a physician and completing the evaluation process, feel free to ask the doctor any questions that come to your mind. It will be especially important for you to understand the diagnosis and the proposed treatment method, if any. Be sure to ask whether the physician uses medication to treat attention deficit. There are many people who have a bias that is either pro- or anti-medication. Some doctors medicate all of their patients with attention deficit. Some do not use medication at all. Choose a physician who is objective. Your child may have a very mild case of attention deficit and may not need medication. On the other hand, she may be one of the many who will need medication in order to concentrate sufficiently to succeed in school. You will want your child to have that option.

If you are dissatisfied with either the diagnosis or the indicated treatment, express your concerns to the physician. Perhaps some clarification will give you the answers you need and convince you that you have come to the right place. Should the opposite be true, it may be worthwhile to seek a second opinion.

For example, let's say that you have good reason to believe that your child has attention deficit. A physician or clinical psychologist simply says, "There's nothing wrong with that kid, he's just all boy. We don't need to do any testing." That exact scenario has set up countless children and families for years of stress, disappointment, and failure. It is possible that you are dealing with a doctor who is inexperienced where attention deficit is concerned, and you may need to go elsewhere.

I would also encourage you to be well informed regarding the use of medication. Refer to the information on medical treatment of attention deficit in Chapter Seven of this book, paying particular attention to recommended dosages. Of course, every child is different, and some will need higher dosages than others. But I find that most children respond well to relatively low doses of the stimulant medications and need increased amounts only occasionally and in very small increments as they grow in stature and in body weight.

Let us look at an example. The appropriate dosage of methylphenidate is between .3 milligrams and 1 milligram per kilogram (2.2 pounds) of body weight in a 24-hour period. A 44-pound (20 kilogram) child should require between 6 and 20 milligrams of methylphenidate per day. I stated in Chapter Seven that I find the most beneficial dosage to be between .5 and .8 milligrams per kilogram of body weight. For the 44-pound child, that would calculate out to a recommended dosage of between ten and 16 milligrams of methylphenidate daily.

If your child weighs 44 pounds and the physician plans to start him out on 30 milligrams of methylphenidate per day, ask some questions! If the doctor starts out with an appropriate dosage but makes frequent increases in the amount and gets your child to a level of medication with which you are uncomfortable, voice your concerns then! Unfortunately, there are some physicians out there who view dosage increases as the best method of solving a child's problems, rather than trying a different medication or adding other types of treatment, such as psychological counseling, behavior management, or a peer group interaction program. Occasionally, I get a transfer patient who has just been dismissed from a hospital after having been weaned from a very high dose of a medication. It is not likely that any young child needs to take 100 milligrams of methylphenidate per day, for instance. As a parent, you must be an intelligent consumer in this regard for your child's sake. Learn about the different medications and their recommended uses. Ask your doctor a lot of questions, and, if you are not satisfied, find another physician.

Don't misunderstand me. I am not encouraging you to shop for a doctor like some people shop for shoes, going from store to store and looking for the most stylish merchandise or the best bargain. I am advising you, however, to find a "good fit" in a physician—a choice that is comfortable and has growing room. Find a doctor who will work for you and with you, devoting his energies to the possibly long-term commitment of overseeing the physical and emotional growth of your child.

Help for the Adult with Attention Deficit

As we saw in Chapter Eleven, many of the symptoms of attention deficit persist into adulthood. There are numerous adults who become aware, at age thirty or forty, that ADD has been the cause of all their concentration problems in school, on the job, and in social situations. A lot of these adults are parents of children who are being diagnosed with attention deficit. Because many of these adults have experienced years of frustration and failure, they may be depressed or dependent on alcohol or drugs. Treatment of adults who have attention deficit can be rather complicated and require psychiatric as well as medical therapy.

The good news is that there is help for these adults. If you suspect that you have this problem, you may want to talk to your family physician first. It may be that he or she will be knowledgeable regarding attention deficit and will be able to treat you. Perhaps that doctor will be lacking in information, but will be willing to study the disorder and work with you. Don't be surprised, however, if your doctor does not feel capable of or comfortable with dealing with this problem. You may need to find another physician to treat your attention deficit.

If you have a child who has been evaluated, ask your child's doctor to recommend someone who can help you. Hopefully, there will be a family practitioner, internist, or psychiatrist in your area who treats adults with attention deficit.

Once again, the Association for Children and Adults with

Learning Disabilities may be able to provide you with a list of recommended physicians. Other organizations, such as the Easter Seal Society, may also prove helpful.

Talk to friends whose children have attention deficit, and you will probably learn that some of these adults have concentration difficulties as well. Perhaps some of these parents are being treated for attention deficit and will be able to guide you in finding help.

Other Sources of Assistance

Once you have located an appropriate physician (for yourself, for your child, or for both of you), you will want to be on the lookout for additional support in your community. Since no one treatment will cure attention deficit, you will need all the help that you can get for your child and for the rest of the family as well. There are numerous organizations and publications that serve people with learning problems and parents who need assistance. I am listing some of these resources here in alphabetical order.

ACLD
The Association for Children and Adults with Learning Disabilities may be your best bet. This national organization, founded in 1964, now has a membership of over 60,000, with more than 800 chapters and 50 state groups.

In addition to providing information regarding physicians in the community, the local ACLD chapter may sponsor a parent support group designed to give parents the opportunity to share their experiences and ideas. It can be extremely helpful to talk about your child's problems with someone who understands. Just knowing that other families experience the same frustrations and learning how other people deal with these difficulties can be immeasurably helpful.

Frequently, parent support groups will hold lectures or seminars in which speakers present information on attention problems and other learning disabilities. These talks can be most informative and can serve to acquaint members with various community agencies and resources.

If there is no support group for parents in your community, I would urge you to start one. Talk to a few friends whose children have attention deficit and convince them of the need for such a group. Hold an organizational meeting to determine your goals, and decide on a meeting time and place. Arrange a speaker on a topic that will draw a crowd, such as "How to Help Your Child Make and Maintain Friendships" or "How to Manage a Difficult Child." Publicize the meeting through local newspapers, community and school newsletters, and flyers placed on strategic bulletin boards. Contact school counselors and area physicians who work with parents of children with attention deficit, and ask these professionals to spread the word about your organization. Undoubtedly, the group will flourish and the members will be most enthusiastic about the help, information, and moral support that they receive.

A friend of mine who lives on the outskirts of Austin, Texas, recently organized just such a group. (There was an ACLD support group in town, but they met at a location thirty minutes from her house and on an evening when she could not attend. She felt that there was a need for a group in her area.) There were eight people at the organizational meeting, 13 at the second meeting, and 32 at the third.

This is not to say that every meeting will be well-attended and that all of the members will come each time. As we all know, parents of children with attention deficit experience some unique problems and some stressful situations that may not always allow them the luxury of going out to an evening meeting. Only 15 parents made it to the fourth get-together of the above-mentioned group; however, 33 showed up for the fifth meeting. The support group now has a membership roster of over 50 names, and it continues to grow. The group has chosen to affiliate with Austin ACLD, and the members pay dues that make them eligible to receive state, local, and national newsletters and to attend Austin ACLD meetings.

The Association for Children and Adults with Learning Disabilities also offers help directly to children who have attention difficulties. The organization can be an excellent source of educational tutors, appropriate alternative schools, camps, and recreation programs. Some ACLD chapters sponsor socialization groups for younger children, as well as interaction groups for older children and adolescents. The younger children can obtain important socialization skills that they often miss due to their impulsivity and lack of attention to detail. Older children and adolescents can talk about some of the frustrations that they have shared over the years and how they have learned to cope with their disability and overcome it. Both of these types of groups can be an extremely valuable part of the treatment process. Again, these groups can be found in large umbrella-type organizations such as ACLD, or organized by physicians or psychologists in the community to provide care for these children.

For additional information concerning ACLD, or for help in finding the chapter nearest to you, contact the national ACLD headquarters at 4156 Library Road, Pittsburgh, Pennsylvania 15234. The phone number is (412) 341-1515.

ASSOCIATION OF LEARNING DISABLED ADULTS

This self-help network was founded in 1978 to serve individuals, institutions, agencies, and other associations. The organization seeks to promote public awareness and to provide technical assistance to learning disabled adults. You may write to Association of Learning Disabled Adults at P.O. Box 9722, Friendship Station, Washington, D.C. 20016.

CH.A.D.D.

Parents of children with attention deficit and professionals interested in helping these kids started CH.A.D.D. (Children with Attention Deficit Disorder) in 1987. This nonprofit, tax-exempt organization began as a small support group and grew quickly as news of the meetings spread and other chapters were formed across the nation.

CH.A.D.D. has four primary objectives: (1) To provide a support group for parents of children with attention deficit. (2) To offer continuing education about ADD for parents and professionals. (3) To serve as a resource for ADD information. (4) To assure that the best educational experiences are available for these children, so that their special disabilities are recognized and are handled appropriately by the schools.

Parent volunteers are happy to help you, and CH.A.D.D. has newsletters and other literature available. For more information about CH.A.D.D., write to 1859 North Pine Island Road, Suite 185, Plantation, Florida 33322, or call (305) 587-3700 or 792-8100.

COUNCIL FOR EXCEPTIONAL CHILDREN

This organization, which has approximately 49,000 members in over 950 local groups, was founded in 1922 for educators and others concerned with the education of the handicapped and gifted. Exceptional children are those students who require special services because their instructional needs differ sufficiently from those of average children. They include the mentally gifted, mentally retarded, visually handicapped, physically handicapped, and hearing impaired, as well as students with behavior disorders, learning disabilities, and speech defects.

Council for Exceptional Children champions the rights of these kids to full educational opportunities, career development, and employment opportunities. This organization also provides information to teachers and parents, sponsors workshops and conferences, gives technical assistance to government agencies and officials, and coordinates a political action network to support the rights of exceptional people. The council has a 63,000-volume library, and sponsors the following publications: *Exceptional Children* (six times a year), *Exceptional Children Education Resources* (quarterly), and *Teaching Exceptional Children* (quarterly).

The mailing address for the Council for Exceptional Children is 1920 Association Drive, Reston, Virginia 22091. The phone number is (703) 620-3660.

COUNCIL FOR LEARNING DISABILITIES

Founded in 1967, Council for Learning Disabilities now has over 2,500 members in ten state groups. This organization is for professionals interested in the study of learning disabilities. Programs aim to prepare teachers for working with special children. The council publishes the quarterly *Learning Disability Forum.* The mailing address is P.O. Box 40303, Overland Park, Kansas 66204. The office phone number is (913) 492-3840.

EASTER SEAL SOCIETY

National Easter Seal Society has a three-fold purpose: to establish and conduct programs that serve people with disabilities, to work with other similar agencies, and to publish and disseminate information. Attention deficit is one of many handicapping conditions recognized by the Easter Seal federation of state and local societies. With a goal of helping the handicapped reach their potential, National Easter Seal Society sponsors special programs for children with attention deficit, such as after-school socialization groups, recreational activities, and summer camps.

You may request further information by writing to National Easter Seal Society, 2023 West Ogden Avenue, Chicago, Illinois 60612. You may call the office at (312) 243-8400.

FOUNDATION FOR
CHILDREN WITH LEARNING DISABILITIES

This national service organization is devoted to increasing public awareness and raising funds to support effective programs that address the needs of learning disabled children and their families. FCLD publishes an annual magazine entitled *Their World*, as well as a *State by State Resource Guide.* The address of the FCLD office is 99 Park Avenue, 6th Floor, New York, New York 10016.

NATIONAL ASSOCIATION FOR
ADULTS WITH SPECIAL LEARNING NEEDS

NAASLN is a recently formed associated organization of the American Association for Adult and Continuing Education (AAACE).

The mission of NAASLN is to establish an effective coalition of professionals, advocates, and consumers to provide opportunities for adults who have special educational needs. Most of these opportunities will be in informal settings such as community continuing education programs, medical and mental health facilities, correctional institutions, postsecondary institutions, and rehabilitative services.

To join NAASLN or to obtain information on membership activities or dues, contact Dr. Boris E. Bogatz, Director, PACE; Gallaudet University, 800 Florida Avenue NE, Washington, D.C. 20002. The phone number is (202) 651-5044 (Voice/TDD).

NATIONAL COMMITTEE
FOR CITIZENS IN EDUCATION
NCCE was founded in 1962 and now has approximately 250 parent networks. Until 1973, NCCE was called the National Committee for the Support of Public Schools. This organization seeks to promote the participation of citizens and parents in all educational issues. NCCE conducts research, distributes information to citizen and parent groups, and studies the extent of citizen and parent involvement in federal education programs. Publications of NCCE include the following: *NETWORK* newspaper (six times a year), handbooks, and pamphlets.

Call toll free (800) NET-WORK for advice and information on educational concerns in public schools. You may write to the National Committee for Citizens in Education at 10840 Little Patuxent Parkway, Suite 301, Columbia, Maryland 21044.

PARENTS ANONYMOUS
Help is available for parents who have trouble controlling their tempers when dealing with their children. If you have been spanking your child very often or very hard, or if you are afraid that you will lose your self-control the next time your kid misbehaves, call Parents Anonymous at (213) 410-9732, or write to the organization at 6733 S. Sepulveda Boulevard, Suite 270, Los Angeles, California 90045. Parents Anonymous, which was founded in 1970, has approximately 1,300 chapters with over 10,000 members.

PARENTS WITHOUT PARTNERS

PWP, founded in 1957, has over 170,000 members in approximately 800 local groups. This organization studies and seeks to alleviate the problems of single parents regarding the welfare and upbringing of their children. PWP also advocates society's acceptance of single parents and their children. Resources available through PWP include referrals to assistance sources, a referral list for child support enforcement, and fathers' rights assistance. You may call Parents Without Partners toll free at (800) 638-8078. The organization's mailing address is 8807 Colesville Road, Silver Spring, Maryland 20910.

POSTSECONDARY LD NETWORK NEWS

Published three times a year by the Learning Disability College Unit of the University of Connecticut, this newsletter includes the latest information on conferences and resources for service providers for learning disabled (LD) students. For additional information about easing the transition to college for learning disabled students, write to the University of Connecticut Special Education Center, U-64, 249 Glenbrook Road, Storrs, Connecticut 06269-2064. You may call the LD unit at (203) 486-4036.

TOUGHLOVE

This network of over 2,000 support groups for parents of problem teenagers was founded in 1977. Toughlove sponsors regional workshops for parents who would like to form support groups. The Toughlove for Kids Program helps kids stay in and complete school. The address for Toughlove is P.O. Box 1069, Doylestown, Pennsylvania 18901, and the phone number is (215) 348-7090.

Avoiding Parental Burn-Out

Let's face it. It is not easy to be a parent—under any circumstances! Your role as the parent of a child with attention deficit may be even harder than that of most parents, because your child is more impulsive, distractible, insatiable, moody, socially immature, and fidgety. Your child probably has very little self-control, and you frequently wonder how to control him yourself.

Parenting can be an exhausting job, and it is essential that you take a break occasionally. Plan to get out with your spouse for a "date" once a week if at all possible. Perhaps you can talk your spouse into covering for you occasionally so you can go shopping or to the library by yourself, or so you can play cards with friends.

If you don't work outside the home and your child isn't old enough for school, enroll him or her in a good preschool or Mother's Day Out program. Don't feel guilty about it. Your child will benefit greatly from the socialization skills that he or she will learn, and you will become rejuvenated and ready to go back to the trenches.

Another worthwhile idea is to form a playgroup for your child. There are several ways to do this, depending on your child's age and schedule. The basic idea is that one mom or dad will care for several children for a few hours one week, and another parent keeps those kids at the same time the next week. This type of setup will give the kids a chance to play with friends and will give parents a breather.

A short vacation away from the kids will do wonders for your morale. If there are grandparents or aunts and uncles who say that they would love to keep your children for a few days, take them up on the offer. The kids will enjoy being in a new environment with doting relatives, and you will be able to get some well-earned rest and relaxation.

Even when you can't get away from it all, there are other ways to escape. Treat yourself to the hot tub, a bubble bath, your soap opera, a movie, a video game, or a good book—while Junior is napping or whenever else you can get away with it. You might even want to take a nap yourself. Don't feel compelled to catch up on the laundry or your housecleaning every time you have a free moment. You definitely deserve a break every day!

A Final Case Study

I would like to end by providing you with one final case study. David came to me as a fifteen-year-old male who was on the fast track to juvenile delinquency. David was failing every subject in school and had very few friends to speak of, except for those with whom he was becoming significantly involved in drugs and alcohol. His relationships with his mother and older sister were quite strained, and he was clearly headed toward being asked to leave home due to the difficulty he was causing. David entered the clinic with a very defiant, angry attitude toward all authority figures, including me.

David had grown up in a small Texas town in a family that was strained by the father's alcoholism and all its accompanying detrimental secondary effects. David had been expelled from two different junior high schools and had experienced several minor altercations with authorities. Upon moving to Austin, David continued to display this type of behavior, showing a general defiance of all adult authority. He was referred to my learning center as a last resort to try to assist him in school before he was completely expelled from the educational system.

David was very standoffish and approached our session with a very hostile, antagonistic manner. Further history identified David as a distractible, socially immature child who never fit in well with his peers and received minimal acceptance from any adults in his life, either at home or at school. David was poorly organized, always lost things, and had a very difficult time keeping anything neat. He never remembered what book or assignment he needed to complete, and he rarely accomplished any meaningful work in the classroom. With his early struggle and lack of success, David began to act out in an attempt to avoid the embarrassment of appearing inadequate before his peers and instructors. With the acting out, the frustration increased, and a vicious cycle developed. Despite this, his mother emphasized (and instructors agreed) that David was really quite bright and capable.

After going over the history carefully, I explained to David the possibilities for his impairment and emphasized repeatedly that some of the difficulty he was experiencing in his learning style may have been beyond his control. I convinced him that it was worth his while to find out the reasons behind his difficulty. And by proceeding with our evaluation, once we accomplished this, there was a good possibility that we could help him with appropriate treatment so that some of these difficulties could be overcome.

David was clearly not impressed, but he was interested enough to agree to the evaluation process. Once this evaluation was completed, it became clear that David indeed had a primary attention deficit that never had been picked up or treated. Although David's intellectual capability was excellent, his achievement (as expected) was notably below his capability. On the neurodevelopmental examination, there were no areas of weakness that could account for this discrepancy between his intellect and his achievement.

With the above results, David was started on psychostimulant medication. He was also given individual counseling to develop his confidence and his ability to feel good about the positive achievements that hopefully would come in the future.

The results of this case are what makes all of the struggles and long hours worthwhile. Here is a young man who had been on an unrelenting track to jail. When I left Austin, David was an honor-roll student and was taking some leadership roles at school. This was clearly as much a thrill to me as it was to David. My last contact with David found him to be a senior in high school, working at a part-time job and planning for college.

I relate this final case to emphasize several points. Obviously, not all cases can end in such a gratifying manner, but each attention deficit child deserves all the expertise, encouragement, and assistance we can provide. Even more importantly, we must help these children believe in themselves so that they can strive to overcome their disabilities.

There are many more Davids who have never been diagnosed and continue down the path to self-destruction. The encouraging news is that we are discovering and intervening in the lives of more and more of these individuals every day. Not all of our efforts prove to be as successful as the one described above, but many times we can make enough of a difference to alter the path and give these individuals a second chance at success.

When children get that chance and receive the proper support, some of their "deficits" may become strengths as they mature. Free flight of ideas may be channeled into creativity, insatiability may breed ambition, and a high activity level may result in great productivity. Some of the very characteristics that are frowned upon in children may be considered admirable in adults. We must help children cultivate these traits and use them to their advantage.

We have more knowledge now than we have ever had and more treatment options. We are clearly achieving greater success than ever before. With continued research we will get even better. Hopefully, this will continue until all children and adults with attention deficit have the same opportunity as anyone else to reach the potential and promise in their lives.

References

CHAPTER 2   CHARACTERISTICS OF ATTENTION DEFICIT

pp. 15–17 Lisa A. Raskin, et al., "Neurochemical Correlates of Attention Deficit Disorder," *Pediatric Clinics of North America*, Vol. 31, No. 2 (1984), pp. 387–396.

CHAPTER 6   ATTENTION DEFICIT PROBLEMS
IN JUNIOR HIGH OR HIGH SCHOOL

p. 70 Melvin D. Levine. *Developmental Variations and Learning Disorders*. Cambridge, Massachusetts: Educators' Publishing Service, 1987.

p. 70 D. P. Hallahan and W. M. Cruickshunk. *Psychoeducational Foundations of Learning Disorders*. Englewood Cliffs, New Jersey: Prentice-Hall, 1973.

CHAPTER 7   THE PHYSICIAN'S ROLE
IN TREATING ATTENTION DIFFICULTIES

pp. 82–84 J. P. Harley, et al., "Hyperkinesis and Food Additives," *Pediatrics*, Vol. 61 (1978), pp. 818–828.

pp. 82–84 K. A. Kavale and S. R. Forness, "Hyperactivity and Diet Treatment. A Meta-analysis of the Feingold Hypothesis," *Journal of Learning Disabilities*, Vol. 16 (1983), pp. 324–330.

pp. 84–85 M. Wolraich, et al., "Effects of Sucrose Ingestion on the Behavior of Hyperactive Boys," *Journal of Pediatrics*, Vol. 106 (1985), p. 675.

p. 85 R.H.A. Haslam, et al., "Effects of Megavitamin Therapy on Children with Attention Deficit Disorders," *Pediatrics*, Vol. 74 (1984), p. 103.

p. 86 S. Sparrow and E. Zigler, "Evaluation of Patterning Treatment for Retarded Children," *Pediatrics*, Vol. 62 (1978), p. 137.

p. 86 American Academy of Pediatrics, "The Doman-Delacato Treatment of Neurologically Handicapped Children." A Policy Statement by the American Academy of Pediatrics, *Pediatrics*, Vol. 70 (1982), p. 810–812.

p. 86 E. Carte, et al., "Sensory Integration Therapy: A Trial of Specific Neuro-developmental Therapy for the Remediation of Learning Disabilities," *Journal of Developmental and Behavioral Pediatrics*, Vol. 5 (1984), p. 189.

pp. 86–87 American Academy of Pediatrics, "Joint Organizational Statement. The Eye and Learning Disabilities," *Pediatrics*, Vol. 49 (1972), pp. 454–455.

pp. 86–87 American Academy of Ophthalmology, "Policy Statement. Learning Disabilities, Dyslexia, and Vision," 1984.

CHAPTER 8   THE PARENT'S ROLE
IN TREATING ATTENTION DIFFICULTIES

pp. 114–115 *Pediatric Behavioral Problems*. Monograph 103. American Academy of Family Physicians, December 1987, p. 25.

pp. 116–117 Ibid.

p. 117 Ibid., pp. 26–27.

pp. 118–119 Jack R. Alvord, "The Home Token Economy: A Motivational System for the Home," *Corrective Psychiatry and Journal of Social Therapy*, Vol. 17, No. 3 (1971), pp. 6–13.

pp. 120–121 *Pediatric Behavioral Problems*, p. 28.

p. 126 Paul A. Boskind, Ph.D., Child Socialization Groups, Participant Handout. Available from Dr. Boskind at Austin Mental Health Associates at Barton Oaks, 901 MoPac Expressway South, Suite 590, Austin, Texas 78746.

CHAPTER 11   ATTENTION DEFICIT PROBLEMS IN ADULTS
pp. 169–171 Steven H. Klee, et al., "Attention Deficits in Adults," *Psychiatric Annals*, Vol. 16, No. 1 (January 1986), pp. 52–56.

p. 171 Frank Wolkenberg, "Out of a Darkness," *The New York Times Magazine* (October 11, 1987), p. 62.

p. 178 Paul H. Wender, et al., "Studies in Attention Deficit Disorder, Residual Type (Minimal Brain Dysfunction in Adults)," *Psychopharmacology Bulletin*, Vol. 20, No. 1 (1984), pp. 18–20.

p. 180 Wolkenberg, p. 66.

CHAPTER 12   FINDING HELP
pp. 188–194 *Encyclopedia of Associations*, 23rd ed., Vol. 1, Parts 1–3, ed. by Karin E. Koek, et al. Detroit: Gale Research, 1988.

pp. 190–191 "CH.A.D.D.: Children with Attention Deficit Disorders," p. 1. Plantation, Florida: More information available from CH.A.D.D., 1859 N. Pine Island Rd., Suite 185, Plantation, Florida 33322.

pp. 192–193 *Postsecondary LD Network News*, No. 7 (1989), p. 4.

p. 193 Ibid.

Bibliography

Abikoff, Howard, and Rachel Gittelman. "The Normalizing Effects of Methylphenidate on the Classroom Behavior of ADDH Children." *Journal of Abnormal Child Psychology*, Vol. 13 (1985), pp. 33–44.

Alvord, Jack R. "The Home Token Economy: A Motivational System for the Home." *Corrective Psychiatry and Journal of Social Therapy*, Vol. 17, No. 3 (1971), pp. 6–13.

Amado, Henry, and Patrick J. Lustman. "Attention Deficit Disorder Persisting in Adulthood: A Review." *Comprehensive Psychology*, Vol. 23 (1982), pp. 300–314.

Aman, Michael G. "Hyperactivity: Nature of the Syndrome and Its Natural History." *Journal of Autism and Developmental Disorders*, Vol. 14, No. 1 (1984), pp. 39–55.

American Academy of Ophthalmology. "Policy Statement. Learning Disabilities, Dyslexia, and Vision." 1984.

American Academy of Pediatrics. "The Doman-Delacato Treatment of Neurologically Handicapped Children." *Pediatrics*, Vol. 70 (1982), pp. 810–812.

American Academy of Pediatrics. "Joint Organizational Statement. The Eye and Learning Disabilities." *Pediatrics*, Vol. 49 (1972), pp. 454–455.

"Attention Deficit Disorder: General Review." *Harvard Medical School Mental Health Letter*, Vol. 2, No. 3 (1985), p. 1.

Audrey, Jann. "My Son Has ADD." *Fort Worth Magazine*, Vol. 2 (February 1988), pp. 14–21.

August, Gerald J., and Barry D. Garfinkel. "Behavioral and Cognitive Subtypes of ADHD." *Journal of the American Academy of Child and Adolescent Psychiatry*, Vol. 28, No. 5 (1989), pp. 739–748.

Baren, M. "The Case for Ritalin: A Fresh Look at the Controversy." *Contemporary Pediatrics*, Vol. 6 (1989), p. 16.

Barkley, Russell A. "An Alert to a National Campaign of Disinformation." *Clinical Child Psychology Newsletter*, Vol. 3 (1988), pp. 1–2.

Biederman, Joseph, et al. "Desipramine in the Treatment of Children with Attention Deficit Disorder." *Journal of Clinical Psychopharmacology*, Vol. 6 (1986), p. 359.

Birmaher, Boris, et al. "Sustained Release Methylphenidate: Pharmacokinetic Studies in ADDH Males." *Journal of the American Academy of Child and Adolescent Psychiatry*, Vol. 28, No. 5 (1989), pp. 768–772.

Bond, William S. "Recognition and Treatment of Attention Deficit Disorder." *Clinical Pharmacy*, Vol. 6 (1987), p. 617.

Boskind, Paul Alan. "Child Socialization Groups." 1989.

Bower, Eli M. *Early Identification of Emotionally Handicapped Children in School*. Springfield, Illinois: C. C. Thomas, 1969.

Brown, Ronald T., and Sandra B. Sexson. "A Controlled Trial of Methylphenidate in Black Adolescents." *Clinical Pediatrics*, Vol. 27 (1988), pp. 74–81.

Campbell, Susan A., et al. "A Multidimensional Assessment of Parent-Identified Behavior Problem Toddlers." *Journal of Abnormal Child Psychology*, Vol. 10 (1982), pp. 569–592.

Carey, William B. "The Difficult Child." *Pediatrics in Review*, Vol. 8, No. 2 (1986), pp. 39–45.

Carte, E., et al. "Sensory Integration Therapy: A Trial of Specific Neuro-developmental Therapy for the Remediation of Learning Disabilities." *Journal of Developmental and Behavioral Pediatrics*, Vol. 5 (1984), p. 189.

Cermak, Sharon A. "The Relationship Between Attention Deficit and Sensory Integration Disorders (Part I)." *Sensory Integration*

Special Interest Section Newsletter, Vol. 11, No. 2 (June 1988), pp. 1–4.

"CH.A.D.D. Children with Attention Deficit Disorders. Hyperactive? Inattentive? Impulsive? Now There's Support for Parents of Children with 'Attention Deficit Disorders.' " Plantation, Florida: 6 pages.

Child Health Encyclopedia: The Complete Guide for Parents. Edited by The Boston Children's Medical Center and Richard I. Feinbloom. New York: Dell, 1977, p. 498.

Christophersen, Edward R., et al. "Explanations for Failures of Time-out." *Pediatric Behavioral Problems*, Table 9, 1987, p. 27.

Christophersen, Edward R., et al. "Using Time-out for Behavioral Problems." *Pediatric Behavioral Problems*, Table 8, 1977, p. 25.

Coleman, William L., and Melvin D. Levine. "Attention Deficits in Adolescence: Description, Evaluation, and Management." *Pediatrics in Review*, Vol. 9, No. 9 (1988), pp. 287–298.

Conners, C. K. "Rating Scales for Use in Drug Studies in Children." *Psychopharmacology Bulletin*, Vol. 10 (1973), p. 24.

Conners, C. K., and E. Taylor. "Pemoline, Methylphenidate, and Placebo in Children with Minimal Brain Dysfunction." *Archives of General Psychiatry*, Vol. 37 (1980), p. 922.

"Consensus Conference on Defined Diets and Childhood Hyperactivity." *Journal of the American Medical Association*, Vol. 248 (1982), p. 290.

Cowart, Virginia S. "The Ritalin Controversy: What's Made This Drug's Opponents Hyperactive?" *Journal of the American Medical Association*, Vol. 259 (1982), pp. 2521–2523.

Crabtree, Loren H., Jr. "Minimal Brain Dysfunction in Adolescents and Young Adults: Diagnostic and Therapeutic Perspectives." *Adolescent Psychiatry*, Vol. 9 (1981), p. 307.

Deuel, Ruthmary. "Treatment of Attention Problems with Stimulant Medication." *The Journal of Pediatrics*, (July 1988), pp. 68–71.

Diagnostic and Statistical Manual of Mental Disorders (DSM III). Washington, D.C.: American Psychiatric Press, 1980.

Douglas, V. I., et al. "Short Term Effects of Methylphenidate on the Cognitive, Learning and Academic Performance of Children with Attention Deficit Disorder in the Laboratory and the Classroom." *Journal of Child Psychology and Psychiatry*, Vol. 27, No. 2 (1986), pp. 191–211.

Dulcan, Mina K. "Attention Deficit Disorder: Evaluation and Treatment." *Pediatric Annals*, Vol. 14, No. 5 (1985), pp. 383–397.

Early, F. "Prevalence of Behavior Problems in 3-year-old Children." *Archives of General Psychiatry*, Vol. 37 (1980), p. 1153.

Encyclopedia of Associations, 23rd ed. Vol. 1, Parts 1–3. Karin E. Koek, et al., eds. Detroit: Gale Research, 1988.

Esman, A. H. "Appropriate Use of Psychotherapies in Adolescents." *Drug Therapy*, Vol. 3 (1981), p. 49.

Farnham-Diggory, Sylvia. *Learning Disabilities: A Psychological Perspective*. Cambridge, Massachusetts: Harvard University Press, 1978.

Feingold, Ben F. *Why Your Child Is Hyperactive*. New York: Random House, 1974.

Feldman, Heidi, et al. "Methylphenidate in Children with Seizures and Attention-Deficit Disorder." *American Journal of Diseases of Children*, Vol. 143 (1989), pp. 1081–1086.

Fine, Benjamin, Ph.D. *Underachievers: How They Can Be Helped*. New York: Dutton, 1967.

Fishbein, Diana, and Jerzy Meduski. "Nutritional Biochemistry and Behavioral Disabilities." *Journal of Learning Disabilities*, Vol. 20 (1987), pp. 505–510.

Fisher, Johanna. *A Parents' Guide to Learning Disabilities*. New York: Scribner's, 1978.

Frank, Yitzchak, and Yocheved Ben-Nun. "Toward a Clinical Subgrouping of Hyperactive and Non-Hyperactive Attention Deficit Disorder." *American Journal of Diseases of Children*, Vol. 142 (1988), p. 153.

Friedman, A. S., and D. B. Friedman. "Parenting: A Developmental Process." *Pediatric Annals*, Vol. 6 (1977), p. 12.

Gardner, Richard A. *MBD: The Family Book About Minimal Brain Dysfunction. Part One: For Parents. Part Two: For Boys and Girls*. New York: Aronson, 1973.

Gauthier, Martin. "Stimulant Medications in Adults with Attention Deficit Disorder." *Canadian Journal of Psychiatry*, Vol. 29 (1984), pp. 435–440.

Gittelman, Rachel, et al. "Hyperactive Boys Almost Grown Up." *Archives of General Psychiatry*, Vol. 42 (October 1985), pp. 937–947.

Golden, G. S. "A Hard Look at Fad Therapies for Developmental Disorders." *Contemporary Pediatrics*, Vol. 4 (1987), p. 47.

Green, M. "When the Toddler Is Out of Control." *Contemporary Pediatrics*, Vol. 1 (1984), p. 86.

Greenhill, Laurence L. "Treatment Issues in Children with Attention-Deficit Hyperactivity Disorder." *Psychiatric Annals*, Vol. 19, No. 11 (November 1989), pp. 604–612.

Hallahan, D. P., and W. M. Cruickshunk. *Psychoeducational Foundations of Learning Disorders*. Englewood Cliffs, New Jersey: Prentice-Hall, 1973.

Halperin, Jeffrey M., et al. "Relationship Between Stimulant Effect, Electroencephalogram, and Clinical Neurological Findings in Hyperactive Children." *Journal of the American Academy of Child Psychiatry*, Vol. 25, No. 6 (1986), pp. 820–825.

Harley, J. P., et al. "Hyperkinesis and Food Additives: Testing the Feingold Hypothesis." *Pediatrics*, Vol. 61 (1978), pp. 818–828.

Hartsough, Carolyn S., and Nadine M. Lambert. "Medical Factors in Hyperactive and Normal Children." *American Journal of Orthopsychiatry*, Vol. 55, No. 2 (1985), pp. 190–200.

Haslam, R.H.A., et al. "Effects of Megavitamin Therapy on Children with Attention Deficit Disorder." *Pediatrics*, Vol. 74 (1984), p. 103.

Hechtman, Lily, and Gabrielle Weiss. "Controlled Prospective Fifteen-Year Follow-Up of Hyperactives as Adults: Non-Medical Drug and Alcohol Use and Anti-Social Behaviour." *Canadian Journal of Psychiatry*, Vol. 31 (August 1986), pp. 557–566.

Hechtman, Lily, and Gabrielle Weiss. "Long Term Outcome of Hyperactive Children." *American Journal of Orthopsychiatry*, Vol. 53 (1983), p. 532.

Hunt, Robert D. "Treatment Effects of Oral and Transdermal Clonidine in Relationship to Methylphenidate: An Open Pilot

Study in ADD-H." *Psychopharmacology Bulletin*, Vol. 23, No. 1 (1987), pp. 111–114.

Ingersoll, Barbara. *Your Hyperactive Child: A Parent's Guide to Coping with Attention Deficit Disorder*. New York: Doubleday, 1988.

Jordan, Nancy C., and Melvin D. Levine. "Learning Disorders: Assessment and Management Strategies." *Contemporary Pediatrics*, (September 1987), pp. 31–62.

Kavale, K. A., and S. R. Forness. "Hyperactivity and Diet Treatment. A Meta-analysis of the Feingold Hypothesis." *Journal of Learning Disabilities*, Vol. 16 (1983), pp. 324–330.

Klee, Steven H. "The Clinical Psychological Evaluation of Attention Deficit Disorder." *Psychiatric Annals*, Vol. 16, No. 1 (January 1986), pp. 43–46.

Klee, Steven H., et al. "Attention Deficits in Adults." *Psychiatric Annals*, Vol. 16, No. 1 (January 1986), pp. 52–56.

Klorman, Rafael, et al. "Effects of Methylphenidate on Adolescents with a Childhood History of Attention Deficit Disorder: I. Clinical Findings." *Journal of the American Academy of Child Psychiatry*, Vol. 26 (1987), p. 363.

Klorman, Rafael, et al. "Stimulant Treatment for Adolescents with Attention Deficit Disorder." *Psychopharmacology Bulletin*, Vol. 24 (1988), pp. 88–92.

Lahey, Benjamin B., et al. "Are Attention Deficit Disorders with and Without Hyperactivity Similar or Dissimilar Disorders?" *Journal of the American Academy of Child Psychiatry*, Vol. 23, No. 3 (1984), pp. 302–309.

Lambert, Nadine M., et al. "Persistence of Hyperactivity Symptoms from Childhood to Adolescence and Associated Outcomes." *American Journal of Orthopsychiatry*, Vol. 57, No. 1 (1987), pp. 22–31.

Levine, Melvin D. *The Anser System: Aggregate Neurobehavioral Student Health and Educational Review*. Cambridge, Massachusetts: Educators' Publishing Service, 1980.

Levine, Melvin D. "Attentional Deficits: The Diverse Effects of Weak Control Systems in Childhood." *Pediatric Annals*, Vol. 16, No. 2 (1987), pp. 117–130.

Levine, Melvin D. *Developmental Variations and Learning Disorders*. Cambridge, Massachusetts: Educators' Publishing Service, 1987.

Levine, Melvin D., et al. *Developmental-Behavioral Pediatrics*. Philadelphia: W. B. Saunders, 1983.

Levine, Melvin D., et al. "Developmental Output Failure: A Study of Low Productivity in School-Aged Children." *Pediatrics*, Vol. 67, No. 1 (1981), pp. 18–25.

Levine, Melvin D., et al. "The Dimension of Inattention Among Children with Social Problems." *Pediatrics*, Vol. 70 (1982), pp. 387–395.

Levine, Melvin D., et al. *A Pediatric Approach to Learning Disorders*. New York: Wiley, 1980.

Levine, Melvin D., and Nancy C. Jordan. "Learning Disorders: The Neurodevelopmental Underpinnings." *Contemporary Pediatrics*, Vol. 4 (1987), p. 16.

Levine, Melvin D., and Frank Oberklaid. "Hyperactivity." *American Journal of Diseases of Children*, Vol. 134 (1980), p. 409.

Levinson, Harold N. *Smart But Feeling Dumb*. New York: Warner, 1984.

Levy, Harold B., M.D. *Square Pegs, Round Holes: The Learning Disabled Child in the Classroom and at Home*. Boston: Little, Brown, 1973.

Lou, H. C., et al. "Focal Cerebral Hypoperfusion in Children with Dysphasia and/or Atttentional Deficit Disorder." *Archives of Neurology*, Vol. 41 (1984), p. 825.

Lozoff, Betsy, et al. "The Mother-Newborn Relationship: Limits of Adaptability." *The Journal of Pediatrics*, Vol. 91, No. 1 (1977), pp. 1–12.

Lyman, Donald E. *Making the Words Stand Still: A Master Teacher Tells How to Overcome Specific Learning Disability, Dyslexia, and Old-Fashioned Word Blindness*. Boston: Houghton Mifflin, 1986.

Mannuzza, Salvatore, et al. "Hyperactive Boys Almost Grown Up." *Archives of General Psychiatry*, Vol. 45 (1988), p. 13.

Mash, Eric J., and Charlotte Johnston. "Parental Perceptions of Child Behavior Problems, Parenting Self-Esteem and Mother

Reported Stress in Younger and Older Hyperactive and Normal Children." *Journal of Consulting and Clinical Psychology*, Vol. 51, No. 1 (1983), pp. 86–99.

Mattes, Jeffrey A., et al. "Methylphenidate Effects on Symptoms of Attention Deficit Disorder in Adults." *Archives of General Psychiatry*, Vol. 41 (1984), p. 1059.

McBride, Margaret C. "Pediatric Pharmacology and Therapeutics: An Individual Double-Blind Crossover Trial for Assessing Methylphenidate Response in Children with Attention Deficit Disorder." *The Journal of Pediatrics*, (July 1988), pp. 137–145.

McDevitt, Sean C., and William B. Carey. "The Measurement of Temperament in 3–7-year-old Children." *Journal of Child Psychology and Psychiatry*, Vol. 19 (1978), pp. 245–253.

McGraw-Hill Dictionary of Scientific and Technical Terms. Sybil P. Parker, ed. New York: McGraw-Hill, 1989.

McGuiness, Diane. *When Children Don't Learn: Understanding the Biology and Psychology of Learning Disabilities*. New York: Basic Books, 1985.

Meller, W., and K. Kyle. "Attention Deficit Disorder in Childhood." *Primary Care*, Vol. 19 (1987), p. 745.

Miller, James S. "Hyperactive Children: A Ten Year Study." *Pediatrics*, Vol. 65 (1977), pp. 217–222.

Mopsik, Stanley I., and Judith A. Agard. *An Education Handbook for Parents of Handicapped Children*. Cambridge, Massachusetts: Abt Books, 1980.

Nemzer, Elaine D., et al. "Amino Acid Supplementation as Therapy for Attention Deficit Disorder." *Journal of the American Academy of Child Psychiatry*, Vol. 25 (1986), p. 509.

Oberklaid, Frank, et al. "Developmental-Behavioral Dysfunction in Preschool Children." *American Journal of Diseases of Children*, Vol. 133 (1979), pp. 1126–1131.

O'Brien, Julie. "National LD Hot Line." *Texas Key* No. 1001 (1st Quarter 1989), p. 7.

Osman, Betty B. *Learning Disabilities: A Family Affair*. New York: Random House, 1979.

Osman, Betty B. *No One to Play With: The Social Side of Learning Disabilities*. New York: Random House, 1982.

Palfrey, Judith S., et al. "The Emergence of Attentional Deficits in Early Childhood: A Prospective Study." *Developmental and Behavioral Pediatrics*, Vol. 6, No. 6 (1985), pp. 339–348.

Paver, Sydney. "Robbie's Morning Tasks." 1989. (Austin Mental Health Associates, 901 MoPac Expressway South, Suite 590, Austin, TX 78746).

Pediatric Behavioral Problems. Monograph 103. American Academy of Family Physicians, December 1987.

Pliszka, Steven R. "Tricyclic Antidepressants in the Treatment of Children with Attention Deficit Disorder." *Journal of the American Academy of Child and Adolescent Psychiatry*, Vol. 26, No. 2 (1987), pp. 127–132.

Plomin, Robert, and Terryl T. Foch. "Hyperactivity and Pediatrician Diagnoses, Parental Ratings, Specific Cognitive Abilities, and Laboratory Measures." *Journal of Abnormal Child Psychology*, Vol. 9 (1981), pp. 55–64.

Postsecondary LD Network News, No. 7 (1989).

Rapp, Doris J., with Dorothy Bamberg. *The Impossible Child: A Guide for Caring Teachers and Parents in School and at Home*. Buffalo: Practical Allergy, 1986. Tacoma, Washington: Life Sciences Press, 1986.

Raskin, Lisa A., et al. "Neurochemical Correlates of Attention Deficit Disorder." *Pediatric Clinics of North America*, Vol. 31, No. 2 (1984), pp. 387–396.

Rosner, Jerome. *Helping Children Overcome Learning Difficulties: A Step-by-Step Guide for Parents and Teachers*. New York: Walker, 1975.

Ross, Linda V., and Edward R. Christophersen. "Grounding as a Method of Discipline." *Pediatric Behavioral Problems*, Table 10, 1985, p. 28.

Ross, Linda V., and Michael A. Rapoff. "Time-out Checklist." *Pediatric Behavioral Problems*, Figure 4, 1987, p. 26.

Satterfield, James H., et al. "Growth of Hyperactive Children Treated with Methylphenidate." *Archives of General Psychiatry*, Vol. 36 (1979), pp. 212–217.

Schuckit, Marc A., et al. "Hyperactivity and the Risk for Alcoholism." *Journal of Clinical Psychiatry*, Vol. 48 (1987), pp. 275–277.

Sebrechts, Marc M., et al. "Components of Attention: Methylphenidate Dosage and Blood Levels in Children with Attention Deficit Disorder." *Pediatrics*, Vol. 77 (1986), p. 222.

Shaywitz, Bennett A., et al. "A Paradoxical Response to Amphetamines in Developing Rats Treated with 6-Hydroxydopamine." *Neurology*, Vol. 26 (1976), p. 363.

Shaywitz, Sally E., and Bennett A. Shaywitz. "Devising the Proper Drug Therapy for Attention Deficit Disorder." *Contemporary Pediatrics*, Vol. 1 (1984), pp. 12–24.

Silver, Larry B. Attentional Deficit Disorder. Booklet for the Classroom Teacher. Ciba, 1987, 10 pp.

Silver, Larry B. "Controversial Approaches to Treating Learning Disabilities." *American Journal of Diseases of Children*, Vol. 140 (October 1986), pp. 1045–1052.

Silver, Larry B. "The 'Magic Cure': A Review of the Current Controversial Approaches for Treating Learning Disabilities." *American Journal of Learning Disabilities*, Vol. 20 (1987), pp. 498–504.

Silver, Larry B. *The Misunderstood Child: A Guide for Parents of Learning Disabled Children*. New York: McGraw-Hill, 1984.

Smith, Helen Wheeler. *Survival Handbook for Preschool Mothers*, Revised and Expanded. Chicago: Follett, 1978.

Solanto, Mary V., and Esther H. Wender. "Does Methylphenidate Constrict Cognitive Functioning?" *Journal of the American Academy of Child and Adolescent Psychiatry*, Vol. 28, No. 6 (1989), pp. 897–902.

Sparrow, S., and E. Zigler. "Evaluation of Patterning Treatment for Retarded Children." *Pediatrics*, Vol. 62 (1978), p. 137.

Speltz, Matthew L., et al. "Effects of Dextroamphetamine and Contingency Management of a Preschooler with ADHD and Oppositional Defiant Disorder." *Journal of American Academy of Child and Adolescent Psychiatry*, Vol. 27 (1988), p. 175.

Sroufe, L. Alan, and Mark A. Stewart. "Treating Problem Children with Stimulant Drugs." *The New England Journal of Medicine*, Vol. 289 (1972), pp. 407–412.

"Sugar Does Not Cause Hyperactivity." *American Medical Writers Association Journal*, Vol. 3, No. 2 (Summer 1988), p. 26.

Taylor, John F. *The Hyperactive Child and the Family, or The Complete What-to-Do Handbook*. New York: Everest House, 1980.

Toufexis, Anastasia. "Worries About Overactive Kids. Are Too Many Youngsters Being Misdiagnosed and Medicated?" *Time* (January 16, 1989), p. 65.

Turecki, Stanley, M.D., with Leslie Tonner. *The Difficult Child*, rev. ed. New York: Bantam, 1989.

Ullman, Rina K., and Esther K. Sleator. "Attention Deficit Disorder Children with or Without Hyperactivity." *Clinical Pediatrics*, Vol. 24 (1985), p. 547.

Ullman, Rina K., and Esther K. Sleator. "Responders, Nonresponders, and Placebo Responders Among Children with Attention Deficit Disorder: Importance of a Blinded Placebo Evaluation." *Clinical Pediatrics*, Vol. 25, No. 12 (1986), pp. 594–599.

Vail, Priscilla L. *Smart Kids with School Problems: Things to Know and Ways to Help*. New York: Dutton, 1987.

Varga, James. "The Hyperactive Child." *American Journal of Diseases of Children*, Vol. 133 (1979), pp. 413–418.

Varley, Christopher K. "A Review of Studies of Drug Treatment Efficacy for Attention Deficit Disorder with Hyperactivity in Adolescents." *Psychopharmacology Bulletin*, Vol. 21 (1985), p. 216.

Varley, Christopher K., and Eric W. Trupin. "Double-Blind Assessment of Stimulant Medication for Attention Deficit Disorder: A Model for Clinical Application." *American Journal of Orthopsychiatry*, Vol. 53, No. 3 (1987), pp. 542–546.

Weiss, Gabrielle, et al. "Hyperactives as Young Adults: A Controlled Prospective Ten-Year Follow-Up of 75 Children." *Archives of General Psychiatry*, Vol. 36 (1979), p. 675.

Weiss, Gabrielle, et al. "Psychiatric Status of Hyperactives as Adults: A Controlled Perspective 15-year Follow-Up of 63 Hyperactive Children." *Journal of the American Academy of Child Psychiatry*, Vol. 24 (1985), p. 211.

Wender, Paul H. *The Hyperactive Child, Adolescent, and Adult: Attention Deficit Disorder Through the Lifespan*. New York: Oxford University Press, 1987.

Wender, Paul H., et al. "Attention Deficit Disorder (Minimal Brain Dysfunction) in Adults." *Archives of General Psychiatry*, Vol. 38 (1981), p. 444.

Wender, Paul H., et al. "A Controlled Study of Methylphenidate in the Treatment of Attention Deficit Disorder, Residual Type, in Adults." *American Journal of Psychiatry*, Vol. 142 (1985), pp. 547–552.

Wender, Paul H., et al. "Studies in Attention Deficit Disorder, Residual Type (Minimal Brain Dysfunction in Adults)." *Psychopharmacology Bulletin*, Vol. 20, No. 1 (1984), pp. 18–20.

Werry, John S., et al. "Imipramine and Methylphenidate in Hyperactive Children." *Journal of Child Psychology and Psychiatry*, Vol. 21 (1979), pp. 27–35.

Whitehouse, Dennis, et al. "Comparison of Sustained-Release and Standard Methylphenidate in the Treatment of Minimal Brain Dysfunction." *Journal of Clinical Psychiatry*, Vol. 41, No. 8 (1980), pp. 282–285.

Wiener, Daniel N., and E. Lakin Phillips. *Training Children in Self-Discipline and Self-Control, or How to Be Good Parents Without at All Times Pleasing, Indulging, or Giving Love.* Englewood Cliffs, New Jersey: Prentice-Hall, 1971.

Winsberg, R., et al. "Is the Dose-Dependent Tolerance Associated with Chronic Methylphenidate Therapy in Hyperactive Children: Oral Dose and Plasma Considerations." *Psychopharmacology Bulletin*, Vol. 23 (1987), p. 107.

Wolkenberg, Frank. "Out of a Darkness." *The New York Times Magazine* (October 11, 1987), p. 62.

Wolraich, M. L. *The Practical Assessment and Management of Children with Disorders of Learning and Development.* Chicago: Year Book of Medical Publishers, 1987.

Wolraich, M. L., et al. "Effects of Sucrose Ingestion on the Behavior of Hyperactive Boys." *Journal of Pediatrics*, Vol. 106 (1985), p. 675.

Woods, David, et al. "The Prevalence of Attention Deficit Disorder, Residual Type, or Minimal Brain Dysfunction, in a Population of Male Alcoholic Patients." *American Journal of Psychiatry*, Vol. 140 (1983), pp. 95–98.

Woods, David. "The Diagnosis and Treatment of Attention Deficit Disorder, Residual Type." *Psychiatric Annals*, Vol. 16, No. 1 (January 1986), pp. 23–28.

Yellin, Absalom M., et al. "Adults and Adolescents with Attention Deficit Disorder: Clinical and Behavioral Responses to Psychostimulants." *Journal of Clinical Psychopharmacology*, Vol. 2, No. 2 (April 1982), pp. 133–136.

Zametkin, Alan J., and J. L. Rapoport. "Noradrenergic Hypothesis of Attention Deficit with Hyperactivity: A Critical Review." In *Psychopharmacology: The Third Generation of Progress*, H. J. Meizer, ed. New York: Raven, 1987, pp. 837–842.

Ziegler, Robert, and Lynn Holden. "Family Therapy for Learning Disabled and Attention Deficit Disordered Children." *American Journal of Orthopsychiatry*, Vol. 58 (1988), pp. 196–209.

Glossary

ADD. Attention deficit disorder. A neurophysiological inability to focus or concentrate.

ADDH. Attention deficit disorder with hyperactivity. A neurophysiological inability to focus or concentrate combined with an excessively high level of physical activity.

AD-HD. Attention deficit-hyperactivity disorder. Term most recently designated by the American Psychiatric Association to refer to attention deficit.

ADD-RT. Attention deficit disorder—residual type. Attention deficit that persists into adulthood.

Allergic rhinitis. Allergy-related inflammation of the lining inside the nose. Condition which, in its most severe form, can share many characteristics of attention deficit due to an inadequate oxygen supply to the brain.

Clonidine. Medication used primarily with children to treat Tourette's Syndrome. Effective in treating certain patients with attention deficit. Is also used to lower blood pressure in adults.

Conners' Teacher Rating Scale. Teacher evaluation of student's academic progress, study habits, and classroom behavior. Used to help identify attention deficit in students.

Continuous Performance Task (CPT). Computerized test used to determine the degree of a subject's impulsivity.

Controlled substances. Medications regulated by the federal government. These are prescribed in controlled amounts with no refills and no telephone orders.

Cylert. Brand name for **pemoline.**

Decoding. The ability to read single words by breaking them down into individual sound units, reblending those sounds, and attributing meaning to them.

Desipramine (Norpramin). Tricyclic antidepressant medication used to treat certain forms of attention deficit.

Dexedrine. Brand name for **dextroamphetamine.**

Dextroamphetamine (Dexedrine). Psychostimulant medication used to treat attention deficit.

Double-blind evaluation methods. Scientific assessment of a therapy involving at least two groups of subjects. No group knows who is actually being treated and who is not.

Dyslexia. A learning disability that prevents normal acquisition of skills needed for reading. There are many possible causes for this disorder.

Dyspraxia. Visual fine motor deficit. Difficulty in looking at something and reproducing it on paper.

Electrocardiogram (EKG). A graphic recording of electrical manifestations of the heart's action as obtained from body surfaces.

Electroencephalogram (EEG). Brain wave test. A graphic recording of electrical discharges of the cerebral cortex as detected by electrodes on the surface of the scalp.

Feingold Diet. A "natural" approach to treating attention deficit by eliminating food colors, additives, and salicylates from the diet. This approach has not proven successful in controlled studies.

Fine motor coordination. Use of small muscle groups to perform tasks such as printing, coloring, cutting with scissors, and tying shoelaces. Some children with attention deficit have trouble with fine motor skills.

Gross motor coordination. Involves use of large muscle groups. Some children with attention deficit have problems with balance, hand-and-eye coordination, and/or judging distance. They may appear clumsy (frequently dropping items, bumping into things, or tripping), or they may have trouble mastering athletic skills, such as throwing, catching, or hitting a ball.

Grounding. A disciplinary technique that teaches a child (approximately age eight or older) the consequences of improper conduct by restricting the child's activities.

Hyperactivity. Excessive physical activity. This may be a physiological problem that belongs to a subset of children with attention deficit, or it may be caused by some other medical condition.

Imipramine (Tofranil). Tricyclic antidepressant medication used to treat certain forms of attention deficit.

Intelligence quotient (IQ). Numerical designation for mental ability expressed as the ratio between an individual's performance on a standardized test and the average achievement according to age.

Learning disability. Significant discrepancy between a child's academic achievement and his or her intellectual capability.

MAO Inhibitors. Medications used as antidepressants for adults. Prescribed for some adults with attention deficit.

Methylphenidate (Ritalin). Psychostimulant medication used to treat attention deficit.

Minimal brain dysfunction, minimal brain damage, and minimal brain injury. Terms used in the past to refer to attention deficit.

Natural consequences. In this context, a form of discipline in which a child is allowed to experience inevitable results produced by nature—not imposed by parents.

Neurodevelopmental assessment. A series of developmental tasks used to evaluate an individual's skills in language, memory, sequencing, visual perception, and fine motor coordination.

Neurophysiological retraining. An approach to treating attention deficit with patterning exercises designed to retrain or reprogram the brain by providing sensory stimuli missed in early childhood. This has not proven to be successful.

Neurotransmitters. Chemical substances that dispatch messages throughout the brain.

Norpramin. Brand name for **desipramine.**

Pemoline (Cylert). Psychostimulant medication used to treat attention deficit.

Petit mal. Seizure disorder that can cause a five-to-ten-second lapse of consciousness. The child may stare straight ahead, making no abnormal or convulsive movements.

Phenobarbital. Medication used to treat seizure disorders. May cause hyperactivity and inattention in some children.

Placebo vs. actual therapy trials. Scientific evaluation in which one group receives a pill that looks like medication but has no effect. The other group receives the actual medication.

Positron emission tomography (PET) scan. Brain scanner that provides sophisticated information about various parts of the brain and their functions.

Primary attention deficit. Attention deficit that is primarily related to a neurophysiological disorder rather than to other secondary problems.

Receptive language difficulty. Slower than normal processing of auditory language (language that is heard).

Ritalin. Brand name for **methylphenidate.**

Salicylate. Chemical related to aspirin that occurs naturally in such fruits and vegetables as peaches, plums, apricots, oranges, grapes, tomatoes, and cucumbers.

Secondary attention deficit. Concentration difficulty experienced in addition to (or possibly made more severe by) a significant learning disability, chronic anxiety state, medical condition, or medically induced reaction.

Sensory integration therapy. Attention deficit treatment approach using techniques that initiate tactile stimulation of areas of the brain to program them to work more efficiently.

Sequencing difficulty. Inaccurate memory of material presented in order (such as days of the week and months of the year). The order is either not appreciated or not remembered. Poor grasp of sequence may cause problems with following multistep directions, with spelling, with arranging words in a sentence, and with putting ideas in a logical order to tell a story.

Standard scientific evaluation. Monitoring of effects and side effects of medication for a specific amount of time.

Statistical analysis. A therapy is examined with careful accounting methods to determine its success rate.

Tegretol. Anticonvulsant medication used to treat seizure disorders. Some physicians feel that this drug improves the concentration in children who have both attention deficit and seizure problems.

Theophylline. Medication used to treat asthma. It has been reported to cause fidgetiness or inattention in some children.

Time-out. Disciplinary procedure used to control problem behaviors in children between eighteen months and ten years of age. Involves placing the child in a quiet, dull setting where he or she can "cool off" and contemplate his or her actions.

Tofranil. Brand name for **imipramine.**

Token economy. Behavior management technique that rewards desirable behaviors through presentation of tokens and punishes unacceptable conduct by withdrawal of tokens.

Tourette's Syndrome. Condition that has characteristics of attention deficit but includes involuntary tics, both motor and vocal. Extremely aggressive behavior is occasionally a symptom as well.

Visual perceptual difficulty. Reversal of letters such as *b* and *d* and words such as *saw* and *was*.

Visual tracking exercise. A controversial therapy using eye exercises and tedious pen and pencil tasks such as mazes to treat various learning disabilities.

Wechsler Adult Intelligence Scale—Revised (WAIS-R). Test most frequently administered for determining adult intelligence.

Wechsler Intelligence Scale for Children—Revised (WISC-R). The most commonly used intelligence test for children between the ages of six and sixteen.

Index

Distractibility, 14–19, 58–59,
144
  limiting classroom
    distractions, 155–156, 157–
    158
  adults, 164–166
Drug abuse, 38
Dyslexia, 36
Dyspraxia, 36

Easter Seal Society, 192
Educational assessment, 30
Elementary school children
    (early grades), 10–11, 55–
    68, 70, 89
  treatment, 95–96
  token economy for, 118
  classroom discipline for, 154–
    159
Elementary school children (late
    grades), 11, 70–71, 148–
    149, 159

Feingold Diet, 82–84
Fidgetiness, 37–38, 69
Foundation for Children with
    Learning Disabilities, 192
Free flight of ideas, 19–21,
59

Grounding, 120–121

High school students, 11
Histories (medical, academic,
    and behavioral), 33–34
Homework, 137–139
Hyperactivity, 3, 10–11, 23–24,
    42–43, 44–54, 69, 100–101
    and sugar, 84–85, 142–143,
    164

Imipramine (Tofranil), 96–97
Impulsivity, 18–19, 59–60, 69,
144
  adults, 167
Inflexibility, 25–26, 49–50
Insatiability, 22–23, 198

Intelligence quotient (IQ), 30,
75–76, 168–170

Junior high school students, 11,
69–80. *See also* Teenagers.

Lead poisoning, 39
Learning disabilities, 35–37, 64–
65, 71–72, 74, 79–80, 133–
134
Listening skills, 157–158

MAO Inhibitors, 179
Medical assessment, 31–33
Medically induced symptoms,
37–38
Megamineral therapy, 85
Megavitamin therapy, 85
Memory (short-term)
    dysfunction, 27, 64, 144
Methylphenidate (Ritalin), 92,
93–95, 100, 101, 104, 186
Mood swings, 26, 69, 96, 102
  adults, 166

National Association for Adults
    with Special Learning
    Needs, 192–193
National Committee for Citizens
    in Education, 193
Natural consequences, 122–123
Neurodevelopmental evaluation,
31–32
Neurophysiological retraining,
86
Neurotransmitter, 14–16, 93, 96,
97

"Paradoxical effect" of stimulant
    medications, 16
Parenting, 4–6, 43–44, 106–128
Parents Anonymous, 193
Parents Without Partners, 194
Performance inconsistency, 24–
25, 76
Phenobarbital, 37